MW01717574

Path to *Enlightenment*

The Seed of Life

Nasrin Safai

BOOK III

Waves of Bliss Publishing

Cover Design: Yantra Design Group, Inc.

Diagrams: James Foster, Theresa Martin, Michael Kopel

Path to Enlightenment, The Seed of Life, Book III. Waves of Bliss Publishing, 2009
ISBN 978-0-9821302-2-3
Library of Congress Control Number: 2008939717

Waves of Bliss Publishing, Jeffersonville, VT 05464 USA
To order books:

Email: Nasrin@WavesOfBliss.com
Website: www.wavesofbliss.com/shop/categories/Books/

Other books by Nasrin Safai:

Gifts from Ascended Beings of Light: Prayers, Meditations, Mantras and Journeys for Soul Growth – Gifts I. Agapi Publishing, 2003.

Gifts of Practical Guidance for Daily Living: Protection, Healing, Manifestation, Enlightenment – Gifts II. Waves of Bliss Publishing, 2005.

Gifts from the Masters of Light: Journeys Into the Inner Realms of Consciousness – Gifts III. Waves of Bliss Publishing, 2005.

Gifts of Wisdom and Truth from the Masters of Light: Tools for Clearing, Release, Abundance and Empowerment – Gifts IV. Waves of Bliss Publishing, 2005.

Path to Enlightenment, The Pillar of Light, Book I. Waves of Bliss Publishing 2008.

Path to Enlightenment, The Golden Throne, Book II, Waves of Bliss Publishing, 2008.

Path to Enlightenment, The Joy of Service, Book IV, Waves of Bliss Publishing, 2009.

Altered States, Biographies & Personal Experience, Body Mind & Spirit, Chakras, Channeling, Consciousness, Awareness & Expansion, Creation Spirituality, Daily Meditation, Everyday Spirituality, God, Meditation & Prayer, New Age, Origin & Destiny of Individual Souls, Science & Religion, Spiritual Teachers, Spirituality, Self Help, The Self.

Printed in the United States of America.

I dedicate this book to the Divine Mother
in gratitude for her motherly care and affection
and her overflowing heart
filled with compassion for all of us.

I dedicate this book to you,
her faithful and devoted children,
who honor her by serving the Light.
May the Seed of Pure and Innocent Life
germinate in your hearts through her Grace.

TABLE OF CONTENTS

KEY TERMS

Chapter I: Protection Grid of Light

- Quotient of Light
- Persistence and Discipline
- Copper Gold Ray
- Turquoise Blue Bubble of the Great Silent Watcher

Chapter II: Healing and Protection

- Feminine Principle
- Red Life Force Energy
- Great Silent Watcher
- Platinum Sphere of Metaron
- Lavender Sphere of Light

Chapter III: Soul Lineage of Light

- Lord Melchizedek
- Melchizedek Brotherhood
- Universal Logos
- Soul Retrieval

Chapter IV: Sphere of Remembrance

- Seventh Ray
- Purple Sphere of Remembrance
- Male and Female Polarities
- Council of Light
- Feminine Angelic Essence of Metatron
- Seventh Golden Age
- Violet Flame and Violet Ray

To Enhance Your Reading Experience

This book is written as a multi-layer exercise. Reading this book affects you at many conscious and subconscious levels. In order to enhance your experience, please follow these recommendations:

Start by saying;

- *"In the name of Light, in the name of the I Am That I Am, in the name of YHWH, in the name of Undifferentiated Source, in the name of Paramatman, in the name of Divine Mother and the Thrones of Absolute, Creation and the Feminine Principle, I ask to receive the highest benefit from this book at conscious and sub-conscious levels. I call upon my Personal Guides and Guardian Angels to be present through the course of reading this book. I invite the Angelic Forces of Light, the Masters of Light and the Great Beings of Light to administer to me the highest benefit from their energy and their teachings through this book."*
- Read the Introduction carefully. Key terms and topics have been explained in the Introduction to enhance your experience of the chapters. Familiarity with these terms can improve your understanding and accelerate your ability to incorporate the teachings in your life. If you walk away with a good knowledge of the Introduction, you would have accelerated yourself on the Path to Enlightenment.
- Keep an open mind. Some of the concepts may be new or different from conventional teachings. If something causes you confusion, continue to read and

be patient. Things are explained in further detail throughout the book. The blanks will most likely be filled in by the time you finish the book. If you need more information to augment what is presented here, please read the books in the *Gifts* series by Nasrin Safai and visit www.wavesofbliss.com.

- It is vital that you begin by reading Book I and II of this series before Book III, as this book is for the advanced seeker on the path to Enlightenment.
- Patience and perseverance are two important qualities for anyone intent on walking a spiritual path. The path of spiritual evolution requires one to contend with a steady climb at the best of times and a roller coaster ride at many others.
- After you read this book from cover to cover, you may still feel that you have not fully understood everything. Do not be concerned, as a period of time for introspection and reflection will bring things into focus. The moment you pick up any one of these channeled books, you begin to walk with the Masters and receive their teachings. At first you may assimilate the materials at subconscious levels. In time, you will begin to consciously understand their wisdom. You may surprise yourself as to how much of this wisdom you retain and use in your everyday life.

I present you with information and materials directly given by the Masters whom I channel. The Masters feel that understanding the subject consciously and energetically through them, as the source, will help the assimilation process. Once you have made your connection with them, they will lead you to more on that subject, when you ask for it. In that way, you will be lead to what is most pertinent and beneficial for you without confusion or delays. However, for those of you interested in reading more on some of these topics, I provide a short bibliography at the end of the book. Some of these external sources have been mentioned in the *Gifts* series books with greater detail at pertinent points in the text.

Most chapters contain exercises which are meant to be repeated for twenty-two days or for the entire month. As you read each chapter, focus on visualizing the components of each exercise and intend that the energy of the grid of Light, candle grid, invocation or the advice given by the Masters stay with you until fully anchored. Intend that you receive everything you need from each exercise. Ask that the Great Beings invoked continue to bless you with their presence and their gifts during and after you read the book. Later, you can go back to those exercises which call to you and perform them for the recommended period of time. Be aware however, that you are accelerating yourself enormously. The information in this book was brought to us in the course of a year. Be patient and gentle with yourself and listen to your instincts. You may need to set the books aside for a while to give yourself a chance to process and to purge. Allow the natural ebb and flow of the energies to help you assimilate the information.

THE GREAT INVOCATION

From the point of Light within the mind of God
Let Light stream forth into the minds of men.
Let Light descend on Earth.

From the point of Love within the heart of God
Let Love stream forth into the hearts of men.
May Christ return to Earth.

From the center where the Will of God is known
Let purpose guide the little wills of men -
The purpose which the Masters know and serve.

From the center which we call the race of men
Let the Plan of Love and Light work out
And may it seal the door where evil dwells.

Let Light and Love and Power
Restore the plan on Earth.

This invocation was channeled through Alice Bailey by the Tibetan Ascended Master Dijwal Khul in the 1940s.

Christ Maitreya, the World Teacher, and the Masters of Wisdom highly recommend that we recite the prayer of The Great Invocation daily. It transmits the energies of great Light, peace and harmony. Christ Maitreya recites the higher dimensional version of this mantra to raise the Quotient of Light for Earth and all souls. For more information, read Transmission Meditation by Benjamin Crème (www.share-international.org).

Preface

The aim of this book, the third in the Path to Enlightenment Series, is threefold; to raise our Light to a Higher Quotient, to maintain that Higher Quotient permanently and to spread this Higher Light, as best we can, in the lower Third Dimensional Reality of earth. The ultimate objective is to bring this entire lower dimensional reality to a higher Quotient of Light. By so doing, we can raise the collective consciousness of all souls and the vibrational frequency of our planet. The overall effect will be to close the gap on the chasm of duality prevalent in our present reality. Living life in duality has become a constant battle between Light and Dark, good and bad, right and wrong, which has distracted us from our true goal, our Divine Mission.

In Books I and II of this series, we gained the knowledge and skills to heal ourselves from the pain and struggles of life in this lower realm. Once we began the healing, our energy bodies started to become strong and stable. This allowed us the ability to raise our personal Quotient of Light and gained us access to the Higher Realms. From the Higher Realms, we can see duality recede and retrieve knowledge which is purer and closer to the Source. From the plateau which we have reached after Books I and II, we must continue to maintain the ability to gain and retrieve knowledge from the Higher Realms directly and rise to higher states.

In his philosophical preamble to *Timaeus,* an acknowledged literary masterpiece, Plato, (427 to 347 BC) makes a distinction between knowledge and opinion and between being and becoming. *Timaeus* is Plato's account of a "teleological Universe", a Universe where things happen in exactly the way it is best to happen, for there is a Higher Power, a *"Designer God, who acts only for the best."* This single power leads us out of chaos into order. (Waterfield. *Plato, Timaeus and Critia.* p. IX)

For as long as I can remember, I have been interested to explore the Higher Realms, connect with the Higher Powers and gain knowledge, "pure knowledge." As a channel, my ultimate goal is to retrieve knowledge directly from the Ascended Masters and Great Beings who reside in these realms. If I relate my life's goal with Plato's example, then it would be true to say that I have been striving to gain the wisdom and the ability to "be" by seeking knowledge from the highest source with the help of the Ascended Masters.

The power to raise our Quotient of Light and the ability to maintain and protect our Light from depletion can pave the path to gain the wisdom of the Higher Realms and use it in this Third Dimensional Reality. This provides the ultimate key to living life in joy while immersed in the thickness of the dross and the density of this Lower Realm. The practical impact of achieving this goal would be the ability to *"live in this world and not of it."* Our attachments to worldly ways and our fears of experiencing pain, trauma, struggles and duality will give way to living life blissfully.

Our focus then shifts from seeing the darkness which surrounds us, to seeing the Light which shines in the world and in each other. A perfect world where we are unaffected by lack of love, for we only see the love that abounds; unaffected by difficulties, for we recognize them as a means of gaining greater strength; unaffected by the actions of others, for we do not take those actions personally but are able to see them as opportunities to express greater compassion. Living life in this state, we become role models for others.

Change Your Attitude

On the first day of one of my week long group workshops, a woman shared with us that she had a difficult time convincing her husband that this workshop would be beneficial to her. His concern was that the events could change her to the point of the breakdown of their personal relationship. A few months later she stopped me before I began another workshop. While she was trying to remind me of her story, the man who stood beside her jumped in the conversation. She introduced him as her husband. I smiled and asked if he felt that she had changed as a result of that workshop. He responded, *"Yes, that is why I am here."* I asked him what had changed; he said the most noticeable change was her attitude. She was calmer, stronger and more confident. She was able to see life in a different light and even laugh at herself and at issues and events which would have upset her before. He summed it all up by saying that she had learned *"not to take life so seriously and not to take events and actions so personally."*

It is my intention to share what has induced positive changes in my life. I leave it up to your free will choices and your individually unique ways to use the material and your own experiences to benefit yourself, others and to serve the Light and the Masters. It is my hope that over time through personal interpretation and empirical knowledge, as well as knowledge you gain directly from contact with the Higher Realms, you too will find a way for the practical expression and dissemination of the teachings to others.

Seed of Life

The subtitle for this book is *The Seed of Life.* This refers to the Seed which holds the Life Force for the entire manifest Creation. This Seed is held in the Divine Mother's Heart. She will bestow this Seed upon those who choose to serve her and in so doing become the Beacons of her Light on Earth. Floodgates of manifestation for material and spiritual abundance can be opened to all who make this choice. Divine Mother has been the Guardian of this Seed from the point where Creation took manifest form. To safeguard the purity of this Seed, Divine Mother has waged many wars against darkness and won many battles on behalf of Light.

Navaratri

It feels serendipitous that completion of this book falls on the 10 day celebration of Navaratri, Divine Mother's victory on behalf of Light in battle with Darkness. According to the ancient Hindu scriptures, the Divine Mother rescued Creation from immersion into darkness in a battle lasting nine days. On the tenth day she gained victory. This entire Creation is an emanation of the Divine Mother's love. This love took form to become the Manifest Creation. She protects her creation from harm by pouring her compassion, grace and mercy upon us. She allows the Creation to become fully manifest in form, by expanding her own essence into multiple layers of dimensionality and matter.

As matter solidifies, resistance grows, for it is the nature of matter and form to offer resistance. The battle of Light and Dark, presented in the Navaratri epic, is this drama enacted. The exact date of the yearly celebration is calculated according to the lunar calendar. It falls around mid-September to mid-October each year. Prayers and meditations offered at the feet of Divine Mother during this time have great potency.

Sri Karunamayi, a living Master states, *"Divine Mother is constantly protecting her entire Creation with the utmost motherly care and affection, but during Navaratri, she showers the whole world with unimaginably radiant energy. To capture this energy and draw it into ourselves, spiritual practices are necessary. As her grace is fully available during this time, devotees of Divine Mother make special efforts during Navaratri to obtain her blessings and as a result make excellent spiritual progress. This time offers us the chance to purify the negative karma of millions of lifetimes, such that tremendous progress can be achieved in a few short days. This is the glory and majesty of Navaratri and it is a precious boon from Divine Mother."* www.karunamayi.org (Newsletter, September 2008)

Three is the number of Creation. The symbol of Trinity is represented in many aspects of our lives. The Triune aspects in the form of Mother, Father, and Child are its essential components. The ancient Hindu traditions honor the Divine Mother's Creative Force in three specific aspects; as the Goddess of Knowledge and Wisdom, Goddess of Spiritual and Material Abundance and Goddess of Destruction and Rebirth; Saraswati, Lakshmi and Durga, respectively.

As Saraswati, Goddess of Wisdom and Knowledge, Divine Mother creates all things. As Lakshmi, Goddess of Material and Spiritual Abundance, Divine Mother sustains all things in abundant forms. As Durga, the Divine Mother moves to the act of destroying the old forms and rebirthing the new so that the grand play of Creation, Sustenance and Destruction begins anew. *Book III* of the *Path to*

Enlightenment series is intended to help us gain the wisdom to create a better tomorrow, the knowledge and the abundance to live a better today and the power to destroy and dispense with all that no longer serves us. The aim is to allow the birthing of a greater future for all.

Nasrin Safai
Stowe, VT
Navaratri Festival, September, 2009

If you love until it hurts,
there can be no more hurt, only more love.

Mother Theresa

Introduction

In my everyday life, I live two parallel realities. One reality is strictly made of the dense matter of this mundane realm and the other is of the subtle and translucent world of the sublime. As a human being in contact with the Ascended Masters in the Higher Realms, I am able to receive information spontaneously while I live in the mundane. As a channel, I receive the information by allowing my body to become the conduit to receive the energy of the Masters. My mind and my vocal chords then become the vehicle for their expression. This means that while I am experiencing life in the mundane, I can also communicate with the Masters to understand the sublime truth hidden behind the mundane.

Over time, I have been able to gather a large body of information from these communications. To grasp the concepts from the Higher Realms and to absorb the wisdom from the Master's requires time, effort and perseverance, both on my part and that of the Masters. The end, however, does justify the means. As we begin to fully apply the knowledge and wisdom held within these truths in our lives, we can move away from the solidity of the dross which our mundane world is immersed in. Gradually, we begin to experience the flow of energy in that same smooth and harmonious manner in our Third Dimensional Realm as in the Higher Realms. Energy follows intent. Clearly defined intentions can become darts of Light which shoot into the darkness of solid matter, illuminating the path and dissolving dross. Enlightenment can be the ultimate outcome.

Soulful Writings

The wisdom and knowledge from the Higher Realms can be dispersed to us in the form of written materials and channeled messages. These messages are filled with the presence, essence, heart and soul of the great beings who offer their own life experiences, knowledge and wisdom to us. These form a body of soulfully written materials which can change our lives by bringing the unknown to the known and making visible what has remained invisible to us for eons of time. As you read these materials, you are bound to have experiences which bring the presence of the Masters more tangibly to you. Any piece of soulfully written material is a multi-layered experience. Some books or articles merit being read many times. We enjoy and learn from them at every reading. When we are ready for a lesson, or for a teacher, that lesson and the teacher manifest along our path. As we grow and learn from a situation, we simply move on to the next step. At each step, the lessons are brought to us and the relevant teachers manifest in one form or another.

Hilda Charlton is a contemporary spiritual teacher who left her body in the early 1990s. In her autobiographical book called, *Hell bent on Heaven,* she tells the story of a book which appeared mysteriously on the shelf, when she most needed it. The book was filled with Master Hilarion's teachings. It became Hilda's constant companion until she internalized its teachings. Then the book disappeared as mysteriously as it had appeared. At that point, the Master himself appeared to Hilda in meditation and began to teach her the Truths as applied in the inner realms.

We have reached a point on our journey together through the *Path to Enlightenment* series where we begin to traverse uncharted territories. This means that you may not find references to these topics elsewhere.

The reason for this may be that those who traversed this path before us chose to keep them hidden as mysteries. It can also be that we are called to be the spearheads to bring this information to the mundane and to anchor it on our personal grids so that it will be posted upon the planetary Grid for others to follow.

Pema Chodron, a contemporary spiritual teacher, in her book, *When things Fall Apart,* states, *"Embarking on the spiritual journey is like getting into a very small boat and setting out on the ocean to search for unknown lands. With wholehearted practice comes inspiration, but sooner or later, we will also encounter fear... Fear is a universal experience... Fear is a natural reaction to moving closer to the Truth... If we want to go beneath the surface and practice without hesitation, it is inevitable that at some point, we will experience fear."* (Chodron, *When Things Fall Apart,* pp. 1, 2)

Merging of the Sublime with the Mundane

Fay came to work and study with me at a time when I was juggling many balls in the air, both in the mundane and spiritual arenas. She was introduced to the Masters at one of my group channeling session. Thirsty for knowledge and longing to remember more, she kept calling me to take her on as a private student or "chela." Chela is a Sanskrit word for student, commonly used to connote a student of the Mysteries by the Masters. I showed resistance and stated that I was unfortunately not available as this was a period of traveling and writing for me. I was settling into a new life which left me with no time or energy for the extensive requirements of working, one on one, with someone who had no prior experience with me or this work. She would not take no for an answer. I therefore agreed and we began. In a short time we had developed a system which suited us both. When I was available, we worked together. At other times, while I traveled, I would provide her with the reading materials and exercises to work with, on her own.

The first few months were rough for both of us. She had too many questions and needs and I had too little time and patience. The primary guide who came during the channeling sessions, as the Master of her Ray and the head of her soul lineage, was St. Germain. He kept insisting that, with perseverance, we will both succeed. He explained that as the learning curve progressed, a point would be reached where she could maintain her Quotient of Light high enough to clearly hear the guidance directly from St. Germain and feel his presence with her. Meantime, I found her lamentations of hardship and lack of direction every time I left town, quite annoying. In one incidence she stopped her meditations while I was gone. She had seen so much Light and felt such a feeling of calm and detachment that she became deeply fearful that she was losing touch with reality.

I confronted her saying, *"Whoever heard of being fearful of Light, calmness and detachment. That was the whole purpose behind meditation."* Self righteously, I stomped away annoyed and angry. That night, in meditation, I flashed back to the memory of an incident which occurred when I was a teenager. I had developed a way to put myself into a trance-like state without realizing that what I did was a form of meditation. During these events I would see profusion of lights and be filled with a sense of peace and calm. As a result, my mind would become clear and I would fall into a blissful state filled with deep gratitude. The prayers and wishes of good will for my friends and loved ones, all souls and all creatures would pour out of me. The intensity of the experience was such that it transcended time and space. When I returned back to the normal state of consciousness, I knew that these prayers were fully received and answered even as they formed in my mind.

One night, while I was deep in process, the room got filled with Light. My eyes were closed at the time and the brightness of the Light made me open my eyes to see if anyone had come to my room and turned on the Light. I saw that the room was filled with Light, without electricity or any other artificial source. I also sensed Angels or Beings whose bodies were emanating Light all around me. I took a gulp of air and froze like a doe bedazzled by the headlights. Unable to breathe in or out, I stayed still in the hope that whatever was the cause of this profusion of Light would disappear and leave without noticing me. After the incident, I stopped meditating for a good long while in the hope that whatever brought that state would fade.

Remembering this event in my own past was a humbling experience for me. It filled me with compassion and the desire to renew my bond with Fay with much greater gentleness. We celebrated the one year anniversary of working together and reminisced about our various moments of agony and ecstasy. It brought me great joy that within a year she had reached the point where she was in direct communion with St. Germain and devoted herself in total service to the Light and the Masters. By now the nature of our relationship had changed dramatically. We were on equal footing, each traversing our parallel paths and coming together once in a while to exchange notes and to commune with the Masters. In the process of serving the Masters, we had learned to befriend each other.

Pema Chodron says, *"When you have made good friends with yourself, your situation will be more friendly too."* To make good friends with ourselves, however, we must be willing to face our fears. That would require courage and honesty. Pema Chodron puts it in perspective by suggesting, *"Getting to know fear, being familiar with fear, looking it right in the eye – not as a way to solve problems but as a complete undoing of old ways of seeing, hearing, smelling, tasting and thinking. The truth is that when we really begin to do this, we're going to be continually humbled."* (Ibid. p. 8)

One day Fay told me that she was looking forward to rescuing her friend from a possible nervous breakdown by helping her make the ever daunting arrangements for her friend's daughter's wedding. I expressed my gratitude in not needing to spend my precious time in pursuit of such unnecessary frivolities. At this, her face went deadly serious and she professed that she used this opportunity to bring the presence of St. Germain and the energies of the Violet Flame to this mundane event, just as she would with any spiritual event. She explained that this was a chance of a lifetime to reach people, places and things which she would not otherwise have access to. She would automatically call the Violet Flame wherever she went and whomever she touched.

She had developed her "auto dial" to the Violet Flame, geared with an instant replay button in her mind. Every person, place and thing would be the recipient of the Violet Ray. *"I am the beautiful being of the Violet Flame,"* was the instant mantra which her mind played in the background whenever she met a person, went to a place or touched a thing. That was another moment of humility and gratitude for me.

It was also a means to free me from my preconceived notion of how spirituality should be brought to others and where, when and how to use the spiritual wisdom. I had explained the qualities of Violet Ray and Flame of Transmutation to Fay. I had brought the presence and energies of St. Germain to her. I had helped her to grow in Light, release her dross and connect directly and personally with St. Germain. But beyond that I had not ventured. She had developed her own way to bridge the gap between the world of the mundane and the sublime.

While stepping up the ladder of spiritual evolution, she had developed her own unique ways to be of service to the Light and to the Masters, especially to St. Germain whose presence and mission plays an invaluable role in the evolution of humankind and Earth. The Enlightenment of all souls and the ascension of earth have a great tribute to pay to the effort of St. Germain at this present juncture of our evolution. St. Germain had the courage to step forward and claim liberty for this land of the "I Am Race" and help build the pillars for the Constitution of the United States of America, while delaying his own ascension to work on behalf of Earth and all souls. In addition to this great service, hundreds of years before, born in different circumstances as Christopher Columbus, St. Germain led the expedition that put the land of the I Am Race, America, on the map of the world.

Pema Chodron says, *"The kinds of discoveries that are made through practice have nothing to do with believing in anything. They have much more to do with having the courage to die. The courage to die, continuously."* (Ibid p.3)

It is in dying to our old ways that we are reborn to the new. The newness of non-judgment, the newness of acceptance, the newness of believing in our own ability to face death and destruction of our ego and to even embark on a head-on collision with our belief systems. Smashing our arrogant beliefs to smithereens may induce pain, but it shall leave us in a powerful and serene state of compassionate acceptance and non-judgment. This is when we are most receptive to change and most likely to learn.

Sometimes it even empowers us to embark upon the unknown. Pema Chodron says, *"Anyone who stands on the edge of the unknown, fully in the present without a reference point, experiences groundlessness."* (Ibid p.2)

That groundlessness is a place where we find ourselves while traversing the Spiritual Path as pioneers. We begin to feel the depth of our divinity when we are able to face ourselves standing at the edge of the precipice. We may be led or choose to venture to the edge ourselves. Yet it is not uncommon to experience fear or reservation when we stand looking from that vantage point at the world. Jumping off that cliff may become a concern even when we know with certainty that it results in the death of the ego and the re-birthing of a union with the Divine.

In *Entering the Castle,* Caroline Myss writes, *"Even as we crave spiritual intimacy with the Divine, however, we also have deep fears about God and the ways that an encounter with the Divine will change our lives. We long for guidance but are terrified of revelation. We pray to know God but fear God's answers. Muhammad, for instance, ran into a cave to hide from the Angel, Allah, sent to entrust him in the service of the Divine. Jesus had to face his fears about his calling."* (Myss, *Entering the Castle,* p.14) She then goes on to tell a story about Graham Greere, a British novelist who waited for three years for an audience with Padre Pio, an Italian Catholic Priest, who died in 1968. Padre Pio carried all the five stigmata's of the Christ on his body. The novelist attended Mass with Padre Pio before his audience and then left before the meeting. His response as to why, was that he was not ready for the way Padre Pio would have changed his life. (Ibid. p. 15)

Myss goes on to say, *"We too, instinctively know that answering a call requires that we have some experience of being reduced to ashes. Whether that is by releasing old wounds or grudges and allowing them to die and be replaced by forgiveness. . .or grieving the death of a loved one and rising out of that into a new life."* (Ibid. p.15)

While we may feel all alone standing at the edge of the precipice, we must remember that we are held in the arms of the Masters and blessed by their presence by our side. They will lead us, protect us and guide us to fulfill our Divine Mission and to reach our destination as Enlightened Masters. As pioneers, we have to pave the path for the generations of souls who follow us. These souls are destined to be the harbingers of the return of the Purity and Innocence Divinely ordained for earth.

Pure and Innocent Female Child Seed

The Seed of Life also refers to the energy of the Pure and Innocent Female Child which is destined to germinate upon Earth by the grace of Divine Mother and through our efforts and service. This will set the pace for the seeding of a new race and the re-birthing of the Pure and Innocent Female Child who will bless our world, our lives and the lives of many future generations. In channeled messages, the Masters have explained to us that each Seed has a twelve thousand year cycle of germination. This cycle is called a Seed Race. The planning phase for each Seed Race takes a span of approximately three thousand years. We are at the entry point to planning the next Seed Race. The theme for the next Seed Race is Anchoring of Purity and Innocence. The symbolic essence of that purity and innocence is held within the Female Creative Force and the Heroes who will carry this essence are the generations of present and future children of earth, both male and female.

The superheroes are those of us who are paving the path which helps this enormous feat become a reality. What we do in service to Light and Divine Mother not only impacts the next three thousand year span of planning but is the precursor for the following twelve thousand years.

This moment in history is an important landmark point as it simultaneously denotes the final conclusion of the twelve thousand year cycle which we are completing and the planting of the seeds for the next one.

The Divine Mother has offered *"the return to the Purity and Innocence intended in the Original Divine Plan"* to be the Creative expression of Life Force and the experience of the generations of humankind for the next cycle. This can be held in place by the symbolic birthing of a *"Pure and Innocent Female Child."* The last Seed Race, which was planned around this time twelve thousand years ago, carries the energetic signature of the *"Clearly Focused Male Child."* The legend of Isis, Osiris and Horus as the Mother, Father and Male Child aspects, of the Egyptian times bears witness to this event. It denotes the beginning of the present cycle of twelve thousand years, which began around nine thousand years ago. It was reinforced two thousand years ago by the birth of Jesus and the revival of the Trinity of Father, Son and Holy Spirit in the recent history of Earth.

The twelve thousand year cycle before that was during the Atlantean Era, where the Seed was encapsulated and held by the Feminine once again. The fulfillment of the plan for that race was aborted, somewhat abruptly, towards the end. The sinking of the land masses within the continent of Atlantis washed away the cultural, spiritual and technological heritage of that Seed Race. Nevertheless, during that cycle in Atlantis, humanity worked on perfecting the Emotional Body, an energy body that is Feminine or Magnetic by nature. During the present cycle we are perfecting the Mental Body, an energy body which is Masculine or electric by nature. During the next cycle we will be engaged in perfecting our spirit body; spiritual by substance, Magnetic and Feminine by nature.

The germination of the Seed of Life in our hearts will facilitate the return of the Original State of Purity and Innocence with which we will build our spiritual bodies. The outcome can provide the final connection of all incarnate souls to spirit. This will be the end of Duality and the advent of Unity; when humankind can live life in lower dimensional realities equipped with perfect mental and emotional bodies. These bodies will be fully connected to the spiritual body and capable of greater consumption and transmission of Light to the physical body and to Earth. Then we will accomplish an enormous task on behalf of Creation, through the grace of Divine Mother.

This may hammer home the importance of the role which we, the initiates and disciples of Light, play in this grand plan. The expression and connotation of our actions stretch well beyond our present life to many generations of our descendents. While living at this present juncture in time and space, we are holding focus on the thought forms, ideas, designs, and concepts for what will manifest in our world and the world of those who follow us, for many generations to come.

The Seventh Golden Age is called the Age of Itza or Knowledge, according to Mayan prophesies. Its advent coincides with Earth's entry into the Age of Aquarius. The symbolic guardian of this age is the Female

Water Bearer. The Hindu Vedic scriptures state that there are Four Yuga, or Ages contained within a Grand Cycle. Each Grand Cycle begins with the Age of Wisdom and Knowledge, called Satva Yuga, and ends with the Age of Chaos, Ignorance and Darkness, called Kali Yuga.

It is believed that at the end of each Kali Yuga, some force or power, catapults all souls out of the depths of ignorance, darkness and chaos into the Age of Satva, or wisdom, to rebirth a new Grand Cycle.

Spiritizing Matter and Materializing Spirit

Metatron calls the act of moving from the darkness of matter to union in Light, Spiritizing Matter. By Spiritizing Matter, we move from the chaos rampant in the Age of Kali Yuga to the peace and harmony of the Age of Satva Yuga. On the other hand, when we leave the Age of Satva and the Light of Spirit to further immerse ourselves into the world of Matter, we are Materializing Spirit. We do this in order to bring the wisdom, peace and harmony of Satva Yoga to the mundane world of matter.

It is Metatron's firm conviction that to simply do one or the other will not suffice any longer. For thousands of years, the focus has been on Spiritizing Matter. This means that we come to Earth, take a physical body and work our way out of the body to return to spirit, leaving this dense realm of Earthly duality behind. He states that to end duality, return to Unity and maintain that Union, once and for all, we must learn to Spiritize Matter and Materialize Spirit simultaneously. Spiritizing Matter will move the matter into the Realm of Spirit, Materializing Spirit will bring spirit into the Realm of Matter. We will not just spiritize the matter of our physical bodies and then leave the planet, but stay here long enough to materialize the essence of that spirit back into the dense body of Earth's matter. Metatron maintains that we need both to accomplish the ultimate task. It is his desire to teach us to do both. This is an unprecedented event which will bring Unity to Earth and take duality out of the picture once and for all.

Quotient of Light

Metatron has stated, on many an occasion, that at this present juncture of our evolution, Earth is incapable of supporting us in raising our Quotient of Light, for it does not have the resources to do it. Furthermore, when we put in the extra effort to raise our own Quotient of Light, the Earth does not have the means to help us maintain it. This is because Earth and the Four Base Elements are so deeply immersed in the density of the Third Dimensional Realm that they have not only lost their elasticity but have gained rigidity. They are only capable of supporting us with the same dim level of Light prevalent on Earth.

The good news is that things are changing rapidly. The Masters of Light are greatly impacting Earth and humanity to release darkness and return to Light. With their help, in the last few decades we have come a long way in raising our own Quotient of Light and propelling ourselves to greater spiritual evolution. We and the Masters have also been instrumental in raising Earth's Quotient of Light by some modest increments. These increments, although small, have been sufficient to facilitate the awakening of a great many spiritually un-awakened souls and furthering the growth of many awakened souls. All of this is a great feat of achievement on our part and a big feather in the cap of all the Masters.

With all that under our belt, we are now at the brink of a major acceleration process and an enormous positive shift. Persistence and discipline are two important qualities as we begin to gain momentum in order to catapult ourselves out of the darkness and the density of lower realms. We need discipline to keep a consistent pace at increasing our Light. While each of us in our own unique way establish ourselves in greater Light, we gain momentum. Persistence is the key for this gain as the pace will be slow and gradual at first.

As our numbers increase and our collective Light becomes brighter, we will become a much greater influence to impact the Five Elements and raise the Light Quotient for Earth and all souls. Then we will become more powerful in accelerating the pace of change. We will be able to move the collective consciousness of all souls to rise in Light, helping Earth to become capable of supporting them. I do not include us in that equation simply because by then, of course, our Light would have increased to much higher levels. Instead of waiting to be supported by Earth and the Five Elements, we become the self empowered Light Beings who take control of, not only our own destiny, but also the destiny of Earth and all souls.

We will continue to be the Beacons of Light who have the power and might to influence both our immediate and greater environment. We are changing the destiny of our Seed Race from one of passive compliance to active participation. This can then become the chosen destiny for the entire collective consciousness of all souls and Earth. Then the duality of Dark and Light will not cause us constant distraction from our path and the density of the third dimensional reality will not be a hurdle. Acceleration to the ever present state of God-Unity is facilitated as a result. It is obvious that maintaining our Quotient of Light is critical and to do this we must understand the significance of protection.

Protection

As we gain greater Quotients of Light, our energetic bodies begin to expand and their substance becomes more ethereal. This is how Light impacts all things. By its nature, Light is a lighter substance than the dark fabric of matter. Our energy bodies will therefore require greater care and protection for two reasons. One, they are larger and spread to a wider expanse around us and two; they are lighter and therefore prone to absorb the heavier materials from the environment.

This is a dichotomy. On one hand, we need to allow our energy bodies to become more expansive in order to have greater sensitivity to the Higher Realms and to connect to the beings of these realms. On the other hand our expansive energy bodies are prone to pick up greater pollution and dross from our present environment. It is natural that the Five Elements play a balancing act in the game of duality and the interplay of Light and Dark. Nature adjusts itself to constantly stay in balance. If you walk into a place and you are vibrating a higher Quotient of Light than the environment around you, the balancing act takes two forms, both of which happen simultaneously: 1) the environment begins to rise in its Quotient of Light, as a result of experiencing your Higher Light; 2) Your Quotient of Light begins to lower as you disperse your higher Light into the environment. These two acts begin to balance the scale until both you and the environment settle down on equal footing, vibrating the same quotient.

While it is our job as the Bearers and Beacons of Light to help raise the Quotient of Light within our environment, to battle single handedly with such situations would be energetic suicide. For as long as our numbers are limited, we must use our Light sparingly. Our work to attain and maintain our own Quotient of Light at the highest possible frequency is a great service to Light, the Masters and ourselves. When we realize the importance of this serious endeavor, we will become vigilant in not only raising our Quotient but also in maintaining it and preventing its depletion at all times.

Your Light may be dimmed dramatically when you are in public places and crowded environments. You experience this in the form of fatigue and low energy. You may have noticed that on the days which you spend in peace and calm in your private and personal space, meditation is easier, energy moves smoother, and work is done with greater ease and grace. On the other hand, a chaotic day spent in a crowded space at the office or in the shopping mall can be exhausting, unless, of course, you create layers of protection around you to prevent depletion of your Light and its disbursement into the environment.

The energies of earth and the Five Elements vibrate closely to the Quotient of Light relevant to the majority of the population of Earth. These are souls who are mostly un-awakened. It is the job of the Five Elements to keep nature in balance and they do not discriminate between a higher Quotient of Light and a lesser one. The earth and the collective consciousness of humankind set the pace. When the collective consciousness of humankind vibrates to a higher scale, the Five Elements adjust the environment accordingly. Based on the prevalent majority, the Five Elements recalibrate the environment to the energy vibration of the masses. The exact Quotient therefore can be lower or higher in different locations, based on the level of Light of the majority in each environment.

The Quotient of Light also varies at different parts of the Globe. Places where nature remains un-tampered and pristine vibrate a much higher Quotient of Light than metropolitan cities and thickly settled towns. Certain sites are vortices of Light and pull a greater Quotient of Light to themselves, attracting people of higher Light to reside there. Other vortices are of darker and dimmer Light and become a cesspool of lower vibrations, attracting chaos and pulling souls with conflictive energies to them.

Various locations on the body of Earth have a distinct beat and rhythm just as the organs of our physical body do. The energetic vibration also changes in critical locations such as North and South Poles and in the Equator. Different continents, countries, states, cities and even villages and hamlets have their own beat, pattern and vibrational frequency. This also translates to one specific locality having a better energy for you at any given moment than another.

As humankind, we are considered to be the species with a higher consciousness; therefore we are the dominant influence in the vibrational frequency of Earth. Having said that, we must also be cognizant of the fact that in each Age and at each Era, Earth pulls to itself the energy of souls with whom it can establish an energetic rapport. Such souls would be attracted to Earth simply because it vibrates to an energy frequency which suits the lessons those souls have chosen to learn while in embodiment.

Protection Grids of Light

In the course of reading each book in the series of *Path to Enlightenment* you come across many Protection Grids. In some of these grids, healing and other qualities are combined with a Protection Grid.

As I have grown in my understanding of the nature of these grids and what they do to assist me in maintaining my level of Light, my appreciation has grown and my discipline in using them has strengthened. I have come to understand that unless I am capable of maintaining my Quotient of Light, I would continue to take a step backward every time I take two steps forward. This, I have painfully noticed, has become a great burden on my already exhausted resources of energy. I notice a significant shift in my energy field when I take a few minutes at the beginning of each day to set up a Protection Grid around me. Invariably, it allows the day to move smoother and my energy to start vibrating at a higher frequency. Protection grids are offered in every one of the books in the *Path to Enlightenment* series. You may choose your favorite ones to exercise daily. Meantime, the most solid and fundamental protection can be experienced by creating a grid formation with the Angels of the Four Directions.

Protection with the Angels of the Four Directions

Uriel, Raphael, Michael and Gabriel are the Archangels who guard the Four Directions together with their Legions. Uriel is the Guardian of North, Raphael of East, Michael of South and Gabriel of West. These four are also the Angelic Forces who are the Guardians of the Throne of God, also known as the Throne of Grace. They possess the might and power necessary to guard the Throne and to withstand the enormity of the Light at the Throne.

The Hierarchy of the Angelic Forces, as described by Prophet Enoch, has seven distinct categories. In order of rank and power, these are Angels, Archangels, Powers, Principalities, Dominions, Thrones, Cherubim and Seraphim. While this may indicate that the Angels and Archangels are the lower rungs of this hierarchy, their power and might is well beyond our human understanding, as their will is aligned with the Divine Will. (Charles, *Book of Enoch*)

Calling upon these Angelic Forces and their Legions will magnify the power and might, as well as the protection afforded to us, exponentially. Simply by calling upon these four at all times can provide us with great acceleration on our path. Their presence with us can help raise our Quotient of Light, for they can impact our bodies and our environment with their Light. They will also help us maintain it by preventing our Light from being depleted or diminished and protect us from all harm and lower vibrational forces and energies. Calling upon them is also an act of service, since it enhances their presence with us and allows greater anchoring of their energies on Earth. Furthermore, we can become the Beacons of their Light, their power and might, allowing them to clear and cleanse Earth, and all souls through us.

A simple, yet potent protection grid, with the help of these four angelic beings, is to visualize yourself facing Archangel Uriel standing in the direction of North, beaming Yellow Light to you; Archangel Raphael standing in the East, beaming Pink Light to you; Archangel Michael standing in the South, beaming Aquamarine-Blue Light to you and Archangel Gabriel standing in the West beaming Emerald-Green Light to you.

Constantly reinforce this visualization by focusing on it. A point will be reached where the process becomes automatic and the presence of the Angelic Forces becomes permanent. Begin practicing this grid of Light formation and you will feel the difference as you build up the energies to reach the permanent state.

Chapter I of this book offers a more elaborate protection grid incorporating the Angels of the Four Directions and their Legions, together with other great beings whose constant presence can be an enormous boost to your spiritual and mundane growth.

The Hierarchies of the Thrones

In books I and II of *Path to Enlightenment,* I referred to Thrones extending from this Third Dimensional Realm of Reality to the 144th Realm of Reality. The Masters have also referred to these realms as dimensions of reality. In this book, I will offer you the hierarchy of the Thrones in sequence as they have been shown to me so far.

The Throne of the I Am That I Am. This is the first Throne, known as the Throne of God in Form. It resides at the 13th layer of Reality. From here on, form becomes less dense and more ethereal.

The Throne of YHWH resides in the 22nd Realm of Reality. The emanations of Golden-Yellow Light brightly illuminate this throne. From here, form is increasingly ethereal moving into Semi-Form.

The Throne of God-Source is in the 33rd Realm of Reality. There is a distinct color vibration of Cobalt-Blue emanating from this throne.

The Throne of Ellah is in the 55th Realm of Reality. This is the half-way point between the realms of Form and Non-Form. Metatron has called this realm the epitome of Semi-Form. White Light emanates from this throne.

The Throne of Undifferentiated Source is in the 108th Realm. At this point, we move completely to Non-Form and Non-Manifest presentation. White Light becomes Pure White Light. Therefore, Brilliant Pure White Light is emanating from this throne.

The Throne of Paramatman is located around the 122nd Realm. By this point, the nature of these realms has turned into pure energy, without substance. These realms are no longer distinctive, one from another. Pure White Light in its pristine form resides here.

The Thrones of the Divine Mother extend from around the 128th Realm and beyond. There are three distinct realms where the Divine Mother roams.

- **The Throne of Absolute** is the residence of the Divine Mother. When brought before this Throne, even though beyond form and substance, we somehow get a sense of a being which is Divine Mother. Her residing realms start from around the 128th Realm and continue stretching to Higher Realms into the Great Silence in the 144th Realm. This is simply an idea from our point of view, since the concept of the existence of realms beyond form is incomprehensible to our mind while we are deeply engrossed in realms of matter and solid substance.

When we visit the Throne of Absolute, the Divine Mother invariably makes her presence and her substance known to us in a form that our minds can grasp. During meditational journeys, we have stood or knelt before Divine Mother at her Throne and received a great many blessings. The Seven Lords of Light and the Maha Lord of Light have their seats at this Throne. There are two layers of reality which stretch beyond this Throne of Absolute.

- **The Throne of Creation** is a pool of Light inside which the Seeds for all thoughts are held. We are brought to the Pool of Creation by the Divine Mother to bathe in the Liquid Light of Creation. Through her grace, we are able to receive the Seeds of thought forms which become the actualization of the manifest reality we choose to co-create and live by.
- **The Throne of Feminine Principle** stretches beyond the Pool of Creation. This is the non-manifest aspect of the Feminine Force. It is an indiscernible experience, incomprehensible in words.

Teachings of the Mystery Schools

In the previous books of this series, I have mentioned Mystery Schools. Such institutions of higher learning have been in place for many thousands of years. Since secrecy was a fundamental requirement, there is no way to know how many may still be active and passing down the wisdom of the Ages.

A Mystery School which started over 2,500 years ago and has continued to make an impact to this day was begun by Pythagoras, the Greek philosopher, mathematician and mystic. He was born Circa 569 BC in Samos, Greece and died about 475 BC. He founded a mystery school in Crotone, what is now southern Italy. The school grew to become a society with an inner circle of followers who lived permanently with the Society and an outer circle who lived in their own houses within the community. Both men and women were permitted to become members of the Society, in fact several Pythagorean women later became famous philosophers. They were all taught by Pythagoras himself while he was alive. After his passing, as society members, they continued to pass on the teachings from generation to generation. The beliefs that Pythagoras held and passed down to his followers were:

1. *That at its deepest level, reality is mathematical in nature,*
2. *That philosophy can be used for spiritual purification,*
3. *That the soul can rise to union with the Divine,*
4. *That certain symbols have a mystical significance,*
5. *That all members of the order should observe strict loyalty and secrecy.*

More on Pythagoras can be found at:
www. groups.dcs.stand.ac.uk/~history/Biographies/Pythagoras.html

Dan Millman, the author of *The Life You Were Born to Live,* which is the contemporary bible for numerological birth charts based on Pythagorean mathematical models, states, *"Pythagoras is best known as a mathematician and one of the founders of Geometry. According to World Book*

Encyclopedia, Pythagoras taught that number was the essence of all things. He mystically associated numbers with virtues, colors and many other ideas." Pythagoras also taught that the Human Soul is immortal. (Millman, *The Life You Were Born to Live.* p.2.)

Pythagoras taught his followers all manner of mysteries through mathematics and numerology. He developed a means to give a numerical value to a soul's mission on Earth based on the numerology of their birth date. Each number from one to nine would have a qualifying objective. For example, three as the number for creation, five as the number for freedom and seven as the number for spiritual fulfillment. He discovered the relationship between mind and matter and the hidden numerical patterns which are keys to unlock the secret mysteries to the human psyche.

The Masters encourage us to use the principles of numerology as described by the teachings of Pythagoras. These teachings have maintained their purity and integrity over the years and are a good source for use in our daily lives. Over the years, the Masters have added their own numerological combinations to make this body of knowledge even more appropriate and applicable to the present Age we live in. By using numbers as their symbols, they can communicate with us and bring our awareness to their presence with us in our day to day experiences. As a general rule, Metatron communicates through number 5 or combinations of 5, such as 555. Sanat Kumara communicates using the numbers 3 and 6, Divine Mother with 3s and 9s, Melchizedek with 4s, Ancient of Days with 7s. Also the Master numbers, such as 11, 22, 33, 44, 55 and so on are ways the Masters communicate. 11:11 is a universal symbol used by all the Masters at this time. Being awakened at 3:33 or 4:44 or 5:55am is also a sign from the Masters.

The Masters have pointed out that among the attributes of the upcoming Seventh Golden Age and the overlapping Age of Aquarius are qualities such as freedom from dogmatic behavior and separation from the dogma of organized religion and secret mystical societies.

In sync with this sentiment, the secret teachings of Pythagoras were recently made public when one of the students attending a present day Pythagorean Mystery School broke his vow of secrecy and published the teachings. A silence of over 2,500 years was broken and the world of scholarly seekers inherited the legacy of Pythagoras. (Ibid)

Throughout the ages, many among the Ascended Masters, from El-Morya and Kuthumi to Hilarion and St. Germain, while in human embodiment have at some point or another been involved in creating Mystery Schools and disseminating their teachings to a select few of their chosen disciples. These same Masters are now beckoning us to come together, tap into those mysteries and free the world of secrecy and secret teachings. Encouraging us, as their present day disciples and students of the mysteries, the Masters are calling us to come together to create Mystery Schools based on their teachings which will help us uplift the consciousness of all souls and do away with keeping secrets.

It must be pointed out, however, that the process of revealing these mysteries must be done in a responsible way. The primary reason why legitimate Mystery Schools keep the mysteries secret is that the information disseminated is very potent and powerful. Such information and meditational techniques, if not applied in the correct order and at the right pace can trigger healing crises and cause confusion and discord. Now is the time that we seek to reveal the mysteries and begin to openly apply the wisdom in a responsible manner in controlled environments; where there is supervision, and in constructive ways to benefit earth and all souls.

Age of Aquarius

A common theme, expressed by adepts in astrology and New Age teachings, is that the Age of Aquarius is a time when humankind takes control of Earth and its destiny. As our rightful heritage, we become the "Sons and Daughters of God" in the course of this Age. Author Vera W. Reid in her book, *Towards Aquarius,* says that the keyword for Aquarius is Enlightenment. The destiny for humankind in the Age of Aquarius is the revelation of truth and the expansion of consciousness. Global crises are attributable to the waning days of the Age of Pisces colliding with the incoming tide of Aquarius. Reid also promotes the idea that some people will experience mental Enlightenment in advance of others and therefore will be recognized as the new leaders in the world. (Reid, *Towards Aquarius*)

Portal Days

Portal days are times when the doorways or portals between our realm of reality and the Higher Realms are open. They are also days when the position of various planets in the heavens create certain alignments or misalignments between the planetary bodies in our solar system. Such positions create a portal between our world and other planetary bodies where exchange of energy is heightened or accelerated. Gateway Portal Days are times when the numerology of the day and the month coincide. There are twelve Gateway Portal Days each year:

1/1, 2/2, 3/3, 4/4, all the way to 12/12. This causes an acceleration of the quality associated with that number. For example, the third of March, or 3/3, is a Gateway Portal Day when the gifts of Creation and Creative Energy pour down. If the number of the year also coincides with the day and the month, the quality is further accelerated for example 9/9/09 is a great Gateway Portal Day of completion, as nine is the number for completion. At the same time 9/9/2007 is an equally important portal day as 2+0+0+7=9. Therefore, the ninth of September of 2007 was a triple completion day.

Another Master number and an important Gateway Portal Day is 11/11/2009, as 2+0+0+9=11. 11 is a Master number. Any number repeated twice brings double strength. Any number repeated three times brings out the gift of the Creative Force for that number. 11/11/2009 is a Portal Day of extreme potency with double creativity in triple strength.

On such intense energy days, connection to the Higher Realms is easier. These are times when you will have a better chance of a clear meditation and clearer connection with the Masters and will benefit from the acceleration which is in process. Prayers, meditations, Light Grid exercises and ceremonies offered on these days will have a much greater impact on these events than on other days. Furthermore, these are days when your body, emotions, mind, soul and spirit need to withdraw from the mundane chores and exercise "being" rather than "doing."

As the planet grows in consciousness, more people become aware of greater energy coming through on portal days. Furthermore, as Earth raises her own vibration, she is communicating at a higher level of consciousness with the other planets in our solar system.

Equinox and Solstice

There are four important portal days which relate to the rotation of Earth around the sun. The natural cycle of Earth's seasons begins with Spring Equinox, which occurs around 19-21 of March, in the Northern Hemisphere. The seasons proceed to Summer Solstice around June 19-21, Fall Equinox around September 19-21 and finally to Winter Solstice around December 19-21 of each year. Obviously, this is reversed in the Southern Hemisphere, where spring is celebrated in September and winter in June.

The three days around each of these events (the day before, the day of and the day after) are important energy portal days as they denote an alignment between our planet and the Sun, allowing a greater energy exchange between the Sun and Earth. Energies are deeply intensified at these times and the manifestation process is accelerated. We can make a point of celebrating these events with ceremonies, prayers, invocations, meditational exercises and candle and Light grid formations.

New Moon and Full Moon Days

The energies are also heightened for a three day period around each new and full moon. These are important days for transmission of energy from other planets. The energy of the Sun is recalibrated through the moon to be transmitted to Earth and to all souls. Those of us, who have reached greater levels of sensitivity to heightened energies, feel these special times with greater intensity. Do not be surprised if you have sleepless nights, headaches and high or low energy experiences in your body around these times. Be gentle with yourself if you have noticed such sensitivities. If you have not, then make a point of checking the calendar to see if your difficult days happen to coincide with new and full moon times. It may ease your mind to know that you are experiencing these symptoms because of your heightened sensitivities and because the Masters are working through you to anchor the energies of the Higher Realms on these special days. Simply knowing this and remembering these special energy days can help you cope better.

Odd and Even Numbered Years

Odd numbered years are Masculine. These are times for action and achievement in the world of the mundane. Even numbered years are Feminine. These are times to turn within and reflect upon our purpose here on Earth and put our attention on the sublime. This therefore implies that our focus naturally turns to achievement in the world of the mundane in odd numbered years and attainments in the world of the sublime and growth in spiritual aspects of our lives in even numbered years. This philosophy is given to us by the Masters in our channeling sessions. Pythagoras also believed in the same principle that odd numbers are Masculine and even numbers are Feminine. http://en.wikipedia.org/wiki/Pythagoras

Numerology of Each Year

In addition to the twelve gateway portal days mentioned, every year has a number of other important portal days that are relevant to that specific year. For example, the numerology of the year 2008 is 2+0+0+8=10. The first energy portal day of this year, therefore, is

01/01/2008. The two other important portal days of this year are 08/08/08 and 10/10/2008 which translates to (10/10/10). In numerology, as taught by Pythagoras, all numbers are summed to make the first nine digits, 1 to 9. Each of these numbers has a specific quality and value. 10 is 1, because 0 does not have numerological value; 11 is 2 (1+1=2); 12 is 3(1+2=3) and so forth.

Numerology of the Year 2010

I find the numerology of the year 2010 intriguing: 2+0+1+0=3. Three is the number for bringing out gifts of the Creative Force. It is therefore Divine Mother's number. Three is also Sanat Kumara's number. Multiples of three of anything bring that energy or event into manifest form and anchor it. Therefore, some of the most important energy portal days in 2010 are 3/3/2010, 3/30/2010, 12/12/10, and 12/21/2010, as the numerological sum of 12 or 21 make 3. At the same time the total number for each of those dates above, add up to a nine which is the number for completion.

Those days in the year 2010 will be great portals of creative energy, impregnated with the power of completion apt to manifest any plan or project through the grace of the combined forces of the Divine Mother and Sanat Kumara.

The Logos

Sanat Kumara is the Logos or "word" for our planet. This reference is also made in *The Bible: "In the beginning was the Word and the*

Word was with God and the Word was God." (John 1:1, *Holy Bible, King James Version*). His Light illuminates our planet as his consciousness envelopes our planet and all souls on earth. As the Planetary Logos, he is our father. He brings our world into Oneness when we awaken to reclaim him as our Logos. He is the King and his Kingdom is the whole world.

Sanat Kumara and his Twin Flame, Lady Venus, reside on the planet Venus. Our Planetary Logos does not reside on Earth nor does he physically visit Earth. This is due to the density and the energetic pollution that Earth has fallen into over the past 18,500 years. Sanat Kumara has told us that he was able to visit our planet in the past, during the height of the great civilizations of Earth.

During the zenith of the Atlantean Era (approximately 50,000 to 30,000 years ago), he came to Earth once a year, to reignite the Flame of God-Unity at the altars of the great Atlantean temples. Before that, during the Lemurian times (approximately 350,000 years ago), Sanat Kumara visited Earth four times a year, at every Solstice and Equinox.

In our channeling sessions, Sanat Kumara has told us that the last time a fragment or particle of his soul essence took physical embodiment to incarnate on Earth, was as Zoroaster or Zarathustra, the prophet of the Ancient Zoroastrian faith. According to Sanat Kumara, Zoroaster has appeared on Earth more than once, the first time was 8,000 years ago to bring the understanding that the duality of Light and Dark are in constant battle over the body of Earth and the consciousness of all souls. He promoted the sacred properties of fire and the importance of placing a sacred Flame upon alters at every home and temple. Even to this day, people of Zoroastrian faith keep fire in a sacred alter in their homes. Sanat Kumara has also informed us that two lesser fragments of his essence came as Zoroaster, approximately 5,000 years ago and 3,000 years ago. This has likely added to the confusion among historians regarding the time of Zoroaster's life on Earth. (Springett, *Zoroaster, The Great Teacher*)

We are fortunate to have a representative of our Planetary Logos alive on Earth at this present time. This is Christ Maitreya, the World Teacher. He is greatly revered and honored by the entire Hierarchy of Masters and Great Beings. Christ Maitreya is a great Master who has already manifested many miracles and appeared in large crowds of people in places across the globe.

He promises to make his presence known world-wide at an appointed time; changing the state of the world and tilting the scale in favor of Light (see Share International at www.share-international.org). Those among Earth's population who have awakened to their own Light shall be his messengers. Sanat Kumara, our Planetary Logos, Lord Melchior, our Galactic Logos, Lord Melchizedek, our Universal Logos and Metatron as the head of the Cosmic Councils, together with the Divine Mother, the Creative Force behind all manifestation, are working through all of us to accelerate the process of Christ Maitreya's appearance worldwide. By raising the Light for the collective consciousness of humankind, we will pave the path for the greater involvement of the World Teacher, Christ Maitreya, in present day world affairs. More can be found on Christ Maitreya in *Gifts from the Masters of Light: Journeys Into the Inner Realms of Consciousness - Gifts III.* Pp 27-42.

Our Star System (or Solar System as it is more commonly known) consists of all the planets and our Sun, the father or godfather for our entire solar system. The residing deities for our Sun are Lord Helios and Lady Vesta. Together they are the Solar Logos for our Star System. Our own galaxy, the Milky Way, consists of many millions of star systems, yet it is still one of the smaller galaxies within our Universe. Our Universe consists of many millions of galaxies. Lord Melchizedek (Mel-Ki-Ze-Dek) is a great being who is the Logos or *"Word"* for our entire Universe. More can be found on Melchizedek in *Gifts from the Masters of Light: Journeys Into the Inner Realms of Consciousness-Gifts III.* pp. 60-74.

Master Thoth, the Record Keeper of Earth

Thoth, also known as Tahuti, is an Atlantean Master and the record keeper of Earth's history for the past 25,000 years. Thoth is also known as the God Mercury, the Guardian of the planet Mercury, and Hermes, God of Magic. *Hermetica,* the teachings of Hermes and *The Emerald Tablets,* the teachings of Thoth the Atlantean, are documents portraying the teachings of this powerful Master. More can be found on Master Thoth in *Gifts from the Masters of Light: Journeys Into the Inner Realms of Consciousness- Gifts III.* Pp. 167-187 and *The Hermetica: The Lost Wisdom of the Pharaohs and The Emerald Tablets of Thoth the Atlantean.*

The Flame of God-Unity

The Flame of God-Unity is our connection with the God-Source. The Spark of Light from God's heart forever burns in our heart and keeps us connected to our Divine Source. This Flame dims and ultimately goes out as human beings forget their Divinity and their hearts become cold and hardened with hatred, fear, forgetfulness and despair.

To awaken to our divinity, we must reignite the Flame of God-Unity in our hearts. Those of us who have always had a special soft spot for God, Angels, Masters and Saints have come to earth with the Flame illuminated in our hearts. This has helped us to remember our divinity and maintain our connection with the Source, yearning to know more and find greater illumination. When the Flame is fully illuminated, we develop a burning desire to know and work with the Angels, Masters, and we tend to be conscious of the needs of others and want to do good for all at all times.

Master Thoth has explained the Flame of God-Unity in this way, *"The Eternal Flame of God-Unity is forever emanating from the heart of the Undifferentiated Source. A spark from this Flame is placed in the Heart Chakra of every soul. When a soul awakens to their divinity, the Flame ignites. When ignited, the Flame of God-Unity is illuminated and awakens the memories of Oneness in your heart."*

Councils of Light

There are Councils of Light presiding over the life and mission of each individual soul. Their purpose is to guide us to our higher purpose, our Divine Mission, and keep us connected to the Source. However, to connect with these councils as awakened souls, we must first fully rekindle the Divine Spark within our hearts through full illumination of the Flame of God-Unity and walk on the path of our spiritual evolution by serving the Light and the greater good of all. We move through the levels of further illumination of the Flame as we become the initiates of the Path to Enlightenment. These levels of initiation put us further on the path to the embodiment of our Divine

Mission. When we begin to live life in full service to the Light and for advancement in that Light, our Councils of Light Members will begin to make their presence known to us. They begin to fully overlight us with their guidance and assistance and help to accelerate us on our Divine Mission and unite us with our entire soul lineage members and the hierarchy of our lineages of Light. This will benefit our souls at a personal level and has enormous planetary impact as well.

Council Members do watch over us, but have no reason to become involved in our mundane life as that is not their particular forte, nor the nature of the service they provide. Their active participation begins when we reach the point where we are able to establish conscious connection with them. This is done as we reach levels of Light that awaken and illuminate the higher chakras above our Crown. This topic will be covered in more detail in *Path to Enlightenment, Book IV, The Joy of Service.*

Framework

In Chapter I, the Divine Mother blesses us with a powerful Protection Grid of Light. It will protect us from lower vibrational energies in our everyday life and help us raise our Quotient of Light to higher levels and maintain it. She asks us to incorporate this Grid of Light into our daily routine; every morning as we wake up and at night before we go to sleep.

In Chapter II, Metatron offers us a grid of Light for healing. Once in a while, the pace of our growth and the stress of our everyday chores come to a clash, wreaking havoc with our nervous system and our emotional, mental and physical bodies. The added pressure of acting in line with spiritual integrity, yet in touch with the mundane reality, can create further stress and occasionally reach the point where our minds and emotions bring us to a grinding halt. For those moments, Metatron offers us this healing grid. The Four Angelic Forces, so important for our growth, stand to protect us while we pull the Red Life Force Energy from Earth and the Pure White Light from Heaven to mix inside our Heart Chakras. This Pink Light becomes the loving balm which can relieve the stress, bring comfort and assist us in healing ourselves to move forward with greater ease and momentum.

In Chapter III, Lord Melchizedek offers us an exercise to connect with our Soul's Mission. He calls upon the Thirty-Three Members of our Soul Lineage for acceleration of our Soul Mission. The Legions of Michael and their Aquamarine-Blue Light of Protection and Mercy are called to watch over us and this grid of Light. Inside the Pillar of Light we journey to the Hierarchies of the Thrones to reach the Presence of the Divine Mother at the Throne of Absolute. The Original Blueprint of the Melchizedek Light is called forth to awaken our DNA structure. The fragments of our soul are called to re-unite as health and wholeness is brought to all soul fragments and personality aspects. Finally, the entire Formation of Light, with the Angelic Forces and the Melchizedek Soul Lineage, is called to continue to pour Light into this grid charging it daily with Light for as long as we choose to receive it.

In Chapter IV, St. Germain offers a grid of Light to connect with the Council of Light. This is an important exercise as it connects us to our Council Members; all of whom are Great Beings of Light ready and willing to assist us in every way possible to accelerate on our path to Enlightenment. Our acceleration also promotes their evolution and ultimate freedom from Earthly realms. By choosing to be our Council

Members, they tie themselves to our life in each incarnation. The Soul Lineage of Light members are called to join the grid formation as we move inside the Pillar of Light to visit the Thrones of the I Am That I Am, Undifferentiated Source and Absolute. The Seven Lords of Light and the Maha Lord of Light join us while we stand in a circle to receive beams of Lavender-Pink-Purple Light from the Angelic Forces of Yahoweh-El.

Chapter V is a Grid of Light given by Quan Yin for us to receive power, purity, love, healing and protection. This Light Grid is accompanied by a candle grid and an applicable ceremony. Quan Yin calls upon Goddess Hecate and Mother Mary to assist in the healing process. The candle grid is given to magnify the impact of the Light Grid, as the candles are imbued with the energies of the three Goddesses. The ceremony is meant to be performed on important Gateway Portal Days, like 1/1, 2/2, 3/3, Equinox and Solstice, as well as other important personal days, such as birthdays or anniversaries. You can do this candle grid for the entire month of your birthday and perform the ceremony on your birthday, offering the healing that is received to be magnified to benefit Earth and all humankind.

Chapter VI offers another Light Grid with an accompanying candle grid by Quan Yin. This one focuses on bringing forth qualities of hope, creativity and happiness. Quan Yin begins by charging our hearts with the Pure White Light of Purity and Compassion. She calls upon a Pillar of Emerald-Green Light, inside of which Christ Maitreya stands. She then invites Archangel Ariel, the Angel of Nature and Creativity, to come forth inside a Pillar of Bright Orange Light to perform a healing on the entire Five Body System and magnify the Light of Creativity within us. Finally, Quan Yin invites us to merge with her, receiving the Light of Happiness and Compassion.

In Chapter VII, Master Thoth offers us a clearing with his Emerald-Green Light of Empowerment. Thoth uses his alchemical powers to bring a healing to our Five Body System and empowers us to be the Beacons of the Emerald Green Light and emissaries of his Light and presence on Earth. We are brought to the inner sanctum of Master Thoth's heart to receive that empowerment. Sanat Kumara then offers us the Lavender Light of the Feminine Creative Force. Through this exercise, we can begin to release all impurities from our energy bodies and the body of our planet, thus promoting our acceleration to greater Light, Joy and Power.

In Chapter VIII, St. Germain offers to place the Sphere of Remembrance in the center of our Heart Chakra. This will bring the memories of our Divinity back to our consciousness. When the Flame of God-Unity is fully illuminated at the center of the Sphere, it becomes the Sphere of Illumination and we become the embodiment of our Divine Self and the reflection of that Divinity.

In Chapter IX is an immensely powerful candle grid offered by Goddess Hecate. She brings forth the energies of Sanat Kumara, Metatron and herself to intercede on our behalf for the release of karma and karmic entanglements. She teaches us to offer what remains of our lives in service to the Light, under the auspices of Christ Maitreya, the Seven Lords of Light and the Maha Lord of Light. This is a potent and powerful grid which can change our lives from a mundane lifetime of swimming in the quagmire of dross and karma to bathing in the bliss of service in the company of Christ Maitreya, The Lords of Light and Maha Lord of Light.

Chapter X, Divine Mother offers us a beautiful Magnification Candle Grid to overlay a new template for a strong and sustaining nervous system and a Five Body System filled with her Light. Magnification Grids combine the energies of candles and crystals to increase the potency of the Grid and accelerate the outcome.

In Chapter XI, Metatron offers to take us on a journey to the Thrones in the Manifest and Non-Manifest Realms of Reality. At the Throne of Absolute, we kneel before the Divine Mother to request a greater future for ourselves, our loved ones and for all humankind. He then calls upon the Blueprint for our Divine Mission to be brought forth and imprinted upon our DNA structure, awakening the memories of our Divine Purpose, at conscious levels.

In Chapter XII, we receive two Abundance Magnification Grids. The first one is offered by Metatron in which we receive abundance from Goddess Lakshmi. In the next grid we invite the Divine Mother in the form of Thirteen Goddesses to intercede on our behalf as we combine this Abundance Grid with the Grid from Lakshmi and Metatron for greater acceleration.

Chakra System

Chakras are energy centers that are located upon a central column along the spine. Most traditional thinking refers to seven chakras which are located in the body. They are, in order from lowest to highest, Root, Sacral Plexus, Solar Plexus, Heart, Throat, Third Eye, and Crown. There are chakras below the Root Chakra which connect us to Earth, and chakras above the Crown Chakra which connect us to the Higher Realms and Heavens above.

Although not traditionally mentioned, there are two other energy centers in the body which the Masters have taught us in our channeling sessions. These are called the Seat of the Soul and the Cosmic Heart. The Seat of the Soul Chakra energy center is located halfway between the Heart Chakra and the Solar Plexus, just below the rib cage. The Cosmic Heart Chakra energy center is located high on your chest and sits over the thymus gland, midway between the Heart Chakra and the Throat Chakra. We continue to refer to the traditional system of Seven Chakras and do not allocate a number for the Cosmic Heart and Seat of the Soul Chakras, yet we place equal importance on them.

The Cosmic Heart is ideally the abode of the Higher Self and our primary connection to the Highest Realms. Due to the drop in the vibrational density of earth over the past 18,500 years, the Higher Self has moved up and resides in the chakras above the body. The Soul, which ideally resides at the Seat of the Soul Chakra, similarly withdrew from the body to sit above the Crown at the 8th Chakra. The knowledge of the existence of these two chakras was lost from common teachings.

However mystics, adepts and high level initiates of the Mysteries are aware of these chakras and exercise energy exchange through these chakras. While we are raising our Quotient of Light and assisting in raising the consciousness of all souls, the Masters encourage us to reignite these energy centers. This will elevate us to higher levels of initiation and accelerate our spiritual growth.

Chakras Above the Body

Chakras eight through twelve extend beyond the Crown Chakra. A cord of Light connects these chakras to the body. This cord is known by various names: Antahkarana is the Sanskrit word most commonly used in the Eastern tradition. The Silver Cord, the Golden Cord, the Cord of Light are other names for this cord. The Masters prefer to call it the Golden-Silver Cord, as it denotes the energetic substance of both masculine and feminine as well as the sublime and the mundane. Metatron speaks of the Golden-Silver Cord as two filaments of Light spun together.

Eighth Chakra, is known as the Soul Chakra where the soul resides. In ideal conditions the soul would reside in the Seat of the Soul Chakra between the Solar Plexus and the personal Heart Chakras. As stated previously, our immersion into the density of the Third Dimensional Realm has resulted in our loosing connection with the soul as an integral part of our being, inside the body. The soul has therefore receded outside the body and fits inside a cocoon or shell at the Eighth Chakra.

Ninth Chakra, is known as the Oversoul Chakra. Connection with the Thirty-Three Members of our Soul Lineage is made through this chakra. The Oversoul carries the totality of the energy of our Soul Lineage of Light.

Tenth Chakra, is known as the Monad. A council of nine members called the Monadic Council resides at the Monad. The nine council members hold the Blueprint and Intention for our individual Divine Mission and higher purpose.

Eleventh Chakra, is known as the Council of Twelve. Twelve Great Beings of Light over-light us through this council. They oversee our spiritual progress and guide us on the path to higher Light. It is their job to connect us with the Divine Mission for our entire Soul Family or Soul Lineage family members.

Twelfth Chakra is where we connect to the Presence of the I Am. Each individual soul has their own representation of God I Am. This representation is considered our Higher Self. We are each a drop from the ocean of the I Am, God in-form. Through our Twelfth Chakra we connect to this essence.

The Perfected Presence of the I Am, God in Form, sits upon a Throne known as The Throne of the I Am That I Am. When the Third Dimensional Realms of Earth were plunged into darkness, we were disconnection from the Higher Realms and the Higher Chakras of our body. The connection to the presence of the I Am, which would normally be through the Cosmic Heart, was severed and the Cosmic Heart Chakra shut down. Our Higher Self then withdrew from the Cosmic Heart and receded to reside in the Twelfth Chakra.

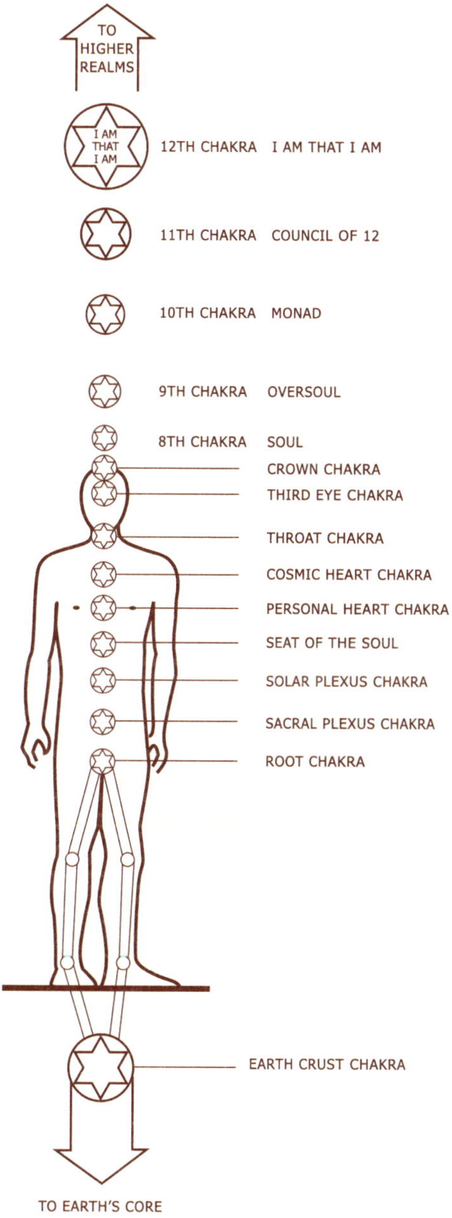

THE CHAKRA SYSTEM

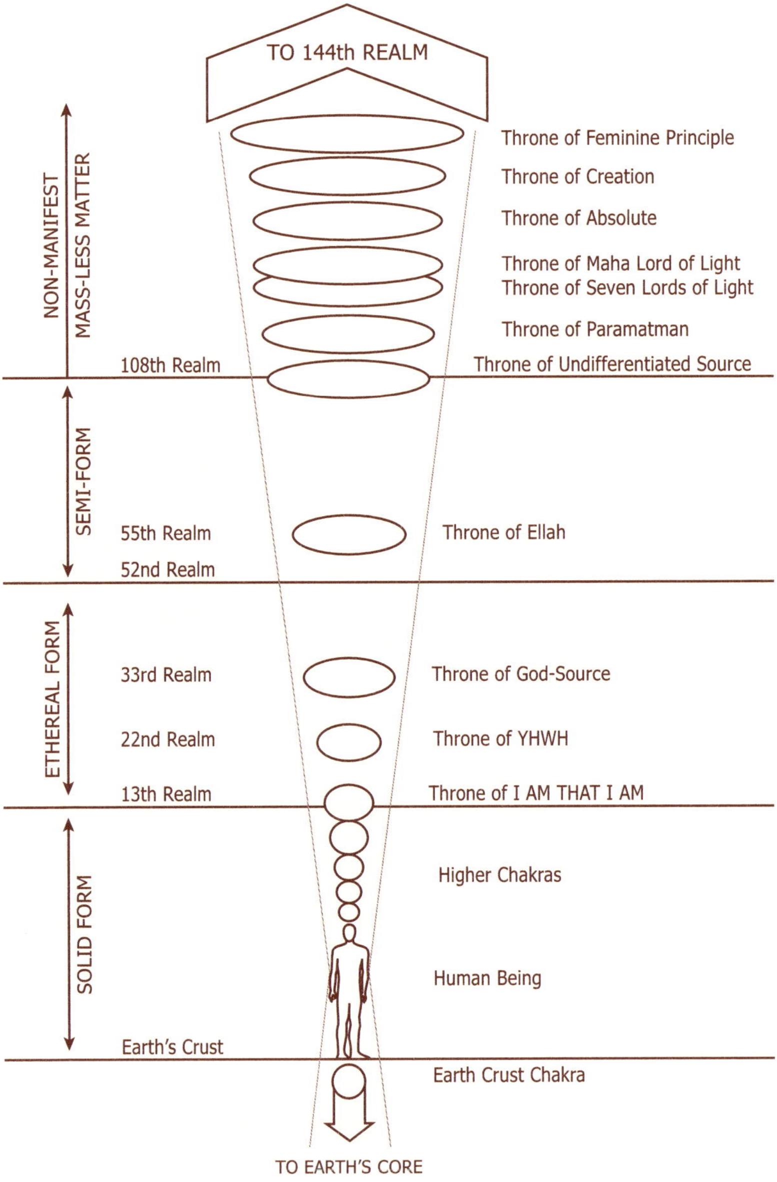

THE THRONES AND REALMS OF REALITY

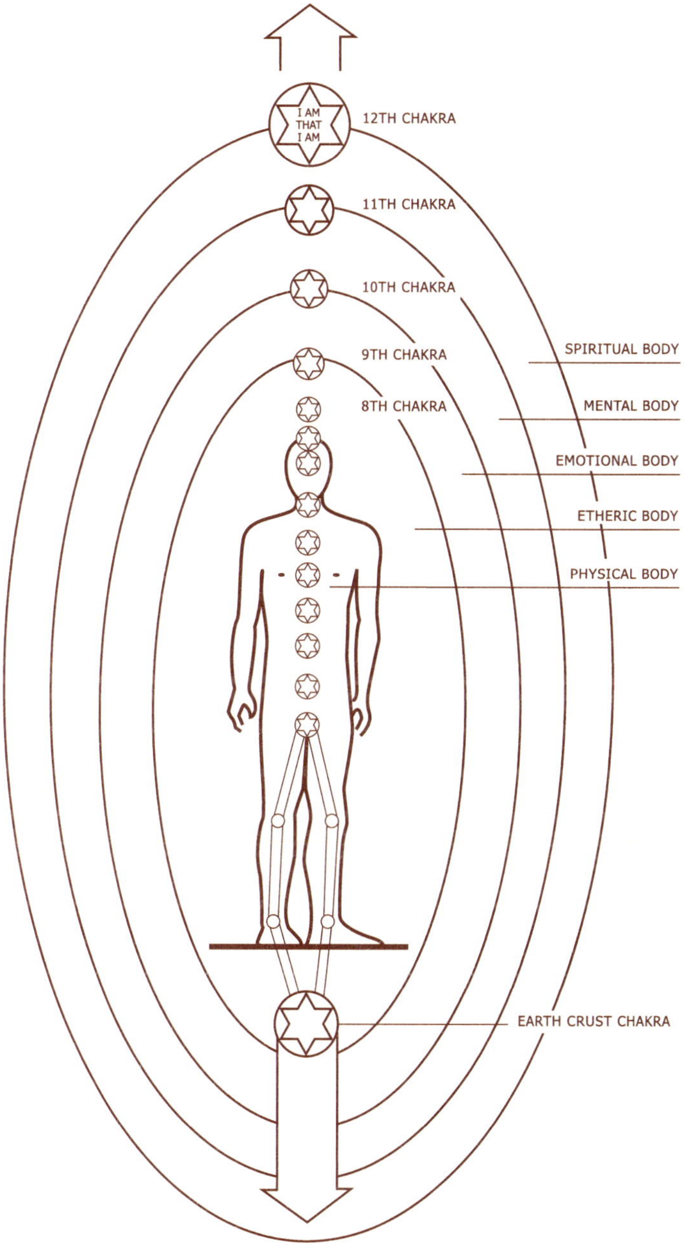

THE FIVE BODY SYSTEM

Chapter Structure

Each chapter begins with an introduction given by me, Nasrin. Then the channeled material begins with each Master identifying themselves with their own special style of greeting. For example, Metatron always begins with, *"Beloveds of my own heart, I am Metatron, take a deep breath with me."* Archangel Michael always greets us with, *"My Brethren of Light, I am Michael."* Jesus always begins with, *"Adonai Beloveds, I am Jeshua Ben Joseph,"* and Goddess Hecate, Quan Yin and Divine Mother always address us by saying, *"My Children of Light, I am Goddess Hecate, Quan Yin or your Divine Mother."*

The channeled material also ends when the Master closes with his or her own special signature closing. This usually occurs at the end of each chapter. Please note these important points in order to distinguish between my introduction and the channeled material.

CHAPTER I

Protection Grid of Light

The Divine Mother has blessed us with a Protection Grid of Light. She has specifically requested that we get into the habit of using this grid as part of our daily routine.

As our Quotient of Light increases, we become more sensitive to energies and less tolerant of lower vibrations. When the environment around us is polluted, it can affect our Light. We work hard to raise our Light in order to be of service to the Masters and to accelerate ourselves on our path of fulfilling our Divine Mission. To keep ourselves at a steady pace of acceleration, we must do as much to maintain our Higher Light as we do to gain that Light. Otherwise, as previously mentioned, we would be taking two steps forward and one step back.

As the collective consciousness of humankind begins to awaken to their spirituality, en mass, they release their dross. This dross can manifest in the form of negative emotions, negative thoughts and all manners of lower vibrational energies. These lower vibrations affect the environment of Earth and the Five Elements. While the majority of people vibrate to these lower energies and adjust to the environment, those who have raised their vibration and their Quotient of Light can be affected negatively.

Our recourse is to form layers of protection around ourselves. This can be done by invoking The Guardian Angels, Angelic Forces of the Four Directions and other Beings of Light to act on our behalf and form layers of protection around us. Divine Mother has therefore brought us this Grid of Light to help maintain the higher vibrational energies around us and to maintain the specific Quotient of Light which we have reached within our auric field.

This particular Grid of Light provides us with healing as well as protection and helps us maintain the higher vibrational frequencies which we have attained through diligent work. We can therefore continue to accelerate without setbacks through this grid.

Set up this grid around your body to protect you from lower vibrational energies and to raise your Quotient of Light to higher levels. By spreading the energy of this grid around yourself, you will begin to receive healing and protection from this moment on. The Divine Mother has asked that you visualize this grid around your body every day as you awaken and reinforce it in the course of the day as often as possible.

Divine Mother's Grid of Protection with the Angelic Forces of Pure White Light

Start your day by standing up, visualizing and calling forth this grid. Call forth Archangels Uriel, Raphael, Michael and Gabriel by standing and facing in their direction as you call them forth. Start by facing in the direction of North. Visualize or say the following out loud,

"I call forth Archangel Uriel to stand in the direction of North, facing me. Uriel is sending me beams of Yellow Light."

"I call forth Archangel Raphael to stand in the East. Raphael is sending me Pink Light."

"I call forth Archangel Michael to stand in the direction of South behind me. Michael is sending me Aquamarine-Blue Light."

"I call forth Archangel Gabriel to stand in the West. Gabriel is sending me Emerald-Green Light."

Return to face the direction of North and continue to create this Grid of Protection. Visualize or say the following out loud,

"I ask the Legions of Uriel to come forth and create a circle around this formation. They stand shoulder to shoulder beaming Golden-Yellow Light to me."

"I ask the Legions of Raphael to come forth and create another circle around the previous one, standing shoulder to shoulder and beaming Golden-Pink Light to me."

"I ask the Legions of Michael to come forth and create another circle around the last and beam Aquamarine-Blue Platinum Light to me."

"I ask the Legions of Gabriel to come forth and create another circle and beam Copper-Gold Light to me."

"I call forth the Legions of Yahoweh-EL to create another circle, standing shoulder to shoulder, and beaming Platinum Light."

"I call forth the Angelic Forces of Pure White Light to create another circle, standing shoulder to shoulder, beaming Pure White Light to me."

"I call forth the Turquoise-Blue Bubble of the Great Silent Watcher to surround all of the circles and fill this grid with Turquoise-Blue Light."

"I call the Angelic Forces of the Violet Ray of Transmutation to come forth and stand shoulder to shoulder forming a circle around the Turquoise-Blue Bubble, beaming the Violet Ray of Transmutation to the entire grid."

"I call the Angelic Forces of the Violet Flame of Transmutation to come forth and stand shoulder to shoulder around the circle of the Angelic Forces of the Violet Ray, the Turquoise-Blue Bubble of the Silent Watcher, the inner circles of the Legions of Uriel, Raphael, Michael and Gabriel, the Archangelic Forces of the Four Directions, and myself in the center. The Violet Ray and Flame of Transmutation seal the entire grid of Healing and Protection."

Pause for a brief moment and bathe in the Energies of Healing and Protection beamed to you from these Great Beings of Light.

While you are facing North say, *"I ask all the Elements, all Beings of Light and Earth in the direction of North for protection and healing."*

Turn clockwise facing East and say, *"I ask all the Elements, all Beings of Light and Earth in the direction of East for protection and healing."*

Turn clockwise facing South and say, *"I ask all the Elements, all Beings of Light and Earth in the direction of South for protection and healing."*

Turn clockwise facing West and say, *"I ask all the Elements, all Beings of Light and Earth in the direction of West for protection and healing."*

Turn clockwise facing north again to complete the circle and say, *"I ask all Angelic Forces of Light, my Guardian Angels and the Elementals in charge of my well being to surround me through this day. I offer this day in service to the Light. So it is. It is done. Amen."*

At first, it may take you a few minutes to complete this protection grid. But after a few rounds you will know it by heart and it will become an automatic part of your daily routine. You may also develop your own routine and add your own intentions and prayers for each day. Soon you will notice a difference.

I have been setting up similar Protection Grids, daily for many years now. It has become a habit. Recently I did a half hearted version at the door just by saying, *"Protection, protection, protection,"* and ran out for the day. By the afternoon, I started feeling nauseous and dizzy. When I arrived back in the evening all the strength had left me. I asked Metatron what was happening to me. He told me that my protection was not put on with clear intent and determination and my energy bodies were wide open. I had cleaned out the dross everywhere and had vacuumed it into my own body. It was wreaking havoc inside me!

He told me to take a salt bath. You may use Epsom Salts or baking soda as a way to cleanse the dross from your body and to clear your chakras while you shower. Using a wet wash cloth you can use the baking soda to rub on all chakras on the front and back of your body along your spinal column. Remember especially your Third Eye and the back of your neck which is the opening to the Channeling Chakra.

"The Aquamarine-Blue Light emanating from the Silent Watcher's Bubble does two things: first, it transmutes any negative energy that may effect and impact you; second, it transmutes any lower vibrational frequencies in your environment that may affect you."

Metatron

CHAPTER II

Healing and Protection

Lord Metatron offers us a grid of healing and protection to nurture our weary bodies, soothe our raw emotions and calm our frazzled minds and nervous systems.

When you feel that your nervous system is under stress and things are getting out of hand; that there are too many events happening around you or you are experiencing general malaise as if you are being spun too fast, use this grid. It is best to perform this grid in the morning and at night to begin and end each day. As we move into accelerated energies, this healing grid will encapsulate and blanket you in the love and compassion beaming from the Archangels, the Legions of Yahoweh-EL, the Great Silent Watcher and Lord Metatron. The emanations of the Healing Rays of Light in this grid are soothing to raw nerves and emotions.

I pray for great acceleration and healing as together we walk the Path of Light in the presence of our beloved Masters.

Healing and Protection Grid

Beloveds of my own heart I am Metatron, take a deep breath with me.

I would like to set up an important energy healing grid for you. This grid is a new healing and protection grid for this year. Every morning use this grid before you begin your day. Train your mind and body to do this exercise as you awaken, before you even get out of bed and every night before you fall asleep. It will boost your energy body and your nervous system. Put this grid around your body, like a Garment of Light. In the morning it will bring you great protection from lower energies and boost your nervous system to cope with the day. At night it will bring you healing; while your consciousness is asleep and does not interfere in the healing process.

Visualize yourself standing inside a Pillar of White Light which brings healing Light and protection to you from the Higher Realms.

It connects you to the Presence of the I Am That I Am and continues to ascend to bring you energies from all the Thrones, reaching to the Throne of Absolute and the Presence of the Divine Mother. Directly below you the Red Earth Energy is rising up to connect with your Root Chakra and to hold you grounded upon Earth. I am going to begin by using the Four Angelic Forces of Uriel, Raphael, Michael and Gabriel. Archangel Uriel stands in the North, facing you, Archangel Raphael is in the East, Archangel Michael is in the South and Archangel Gabriel is in the West.

All Archangels are beaming their specific Light to you. Their hands are held upright with the palms directed at your body. From the palms of their hands and from the center of their Heart Chakra, energy is pouring out to you. This energy moves into your Third Eye Chakra, your Throat Chakra, your Cosmic Heart Chakra, your Personal Heart Chakra, your Seat of the Soul Chakra, your Solar Plexus Chakra, and your Sacral Plexus Chakra. The two energy centers that we will not touch are the Crown Chakra and the Root Chakra. The Root Chakra is directly receiving energy from Earth and the Crown Chakra is directly receiving energy from the Heavens above.

Archangel Uriel is sending you the Yellow Light of Wisdom, the Cosmic Inner Light from the heart core of the Undifferentiated Source, God before it manifested in Form. Archangel Raphael is beaming to you the Pink Light of Divine Love, the Light of Healing and Compassion. This is energy of the Feminine Principle. Therefore, the Divine Mother in two of her forms, as Mother Mary and as Quan Yin, is also behind this Pink Light. Archangel Michael is sending you his Aquamarine-Blue Light of Protection. This Light has the power to protect and to transmute all harm. Archangel Gabriel is sending you the

Emerald-Green Healing Light of Truth to bring physical, emotional and mental healing. Take a deep breath.

Bathe in the Light of the Four Archangels while you stand in the Pillar of White Light. Now visualize you are connecting to the Red Life Force Energy of Earth. This Red Energy comes up from the planet and moves up your left foot to your left leg. Moving up into your Root Chakra it crosses over and goes down your right leg. It connects you to the life giving Red Light of Earth. Through your Root Chakra, it then carries the pain, pollution and dross from your body and drains it out of your right foot releasing it back to Earth for transmutation. Now, visualize another beam of Red Energy coming up from Earth but this time entering through your right foot, moving up your right leg. It goes into your Root Chakra and crosses to your left leg and down to Earth. At each given point, there are two streams of energy moving through your legs. One is moving up your right leg going through your Root Chakra and draining out of your left leg. Another is going up your left leg, reaching your Root Chakra, clearing your Root Chakra and draining out of the right leg.

This is an important energy exchange. It connects you to Mother Earth to help you become grounded and to benefit from the Red Life Force Energy of Earth. At the same time, it releases back to Earth the dross, pollution and pain from your Root Chakra which collects the pollution from the chakras above it. Pollution is absorbed from the lower vibrational energies which you encounter each day. The Red Life Force Energy of Earth helps you maintain your connection to Earth. It helps to keep you from becoming depressed, and to prevent you from feeling disconnected. Whenever you feel out of sorts and unable to function, pull the Red Energy up and start this double flow of Red Energy up and down your legs through your Root Chakra.

Bring your attention back to visualize yourself in the center with the Four Archangels around you. Visualize a Sphere of Lavender Light directly outside of the formation of the Four Angelic Forces. The Legions of Yahoweh-EL are standing shoulder to shoulder in the formation of a circle inside of this Lavender colored Sphere. Each of the members of the Legions of Yahoweh-EL become ablaze with Lavender-Pink and Magenta Light. Yahoweh-EL and her Legions are fully illuminated and look like beautiful fairies. Take a deep breath and bathe in the Light of the Legions of Yahoweh-EL and the Lavender Sphere of Light.

Now, visualize a huge Bubble of Aquamarine-Blue Light which covers this entire formation. This Bubble is sent to you from the heart of the Great Silent Watcher, a great Cosmic Being who held the ideal design for this entire Solar System in her own heart until it became manifest. The process took millions of years. She is very patient and very powerful. Calling upon her will take you to a whole new level of healing and a new level of creativity. I ask you to become aware of the Great Silent Watcher. I ask you to start communicating with the Great Silent Watcher. She may present herself in the form of a great huge Cosmic Being, or in the form of huge eyes that appear right in front of you. She may give you your own sign.

The Aquamarine-Blue Light emanating from the Silent Watcher's Bubble does two things: first, it transmutes any negative energy that may effect and impact you; second, it transmutes any lower vibrational frequencies in your environment that may affect you. Your environment consists of the Elements of Earth, Water, Fire, Air and Ether. These Five Elements are responsible for everything manifest. Everything created in form is created with the Five Elements. Imagine the impact when the vibration of the Five Elements is raised. It can raise the vibration of all things. It can also render lower vibrational forces harmless to you. Therefore, no harm can ever come to you in spite of the circumstances. This is the impact of this Blue Bubble. Take a deep breath and bathe in this Aquamarine-Blue Bubble of Light.

Now visualize a Platinum Sphere placed around this entire formation. This is the Platinum Sphere of Protection offered by Metatron. Visualize the outside surface of this powerful Sphere as smooth and shiny. Anything of lower vibration will get reflected back, like a mirror, and does not penetrate inside of the Sphere to you. Feel the energy of this Sphere and allow yourself to experience it. The higher vibrational energies are in harmony with it and therefore, are allowed to penetrate into it. All the good energy that you have raised inside of this grid and the healing transmitted to you from the Angelic Forces remains inside. It does not leak nor does it lose its power or disperse it due to the protective power of the Platinum Sphere of Metatron. Pause, take a few deep breaths and feel this healing protective energy.

I will give you a quick recap. In the morning as you awaken and at night before you fall asleep, establish this grid around you. Visualize yourself standing in the Pillar of Light. Visualize yourself connecting from below your feet to the Red Life Force Energy of Earth. This will energize and harmonize you with the Life Force of Earth and release the dross from your body into Earth for transmutation. Then visualize the Angelic Forces of Yahoweh-El form a circle around you. The Lavender Sphere is formed around you and the Archangels; over that, visualize the Aquamarine-Blue Bubble of the Great Silent Watcher and finally, the Platinum Sphere of Metatron to seal everything within.

When you have completed the formation say, *"This grid will remain charged for the next twenty-four hours."* In this way, if you happen to miss a morning or evening, the grid will continue to be charged until you repeat the exercise.

I am your father Metatron. So it is.

Summary of Metatron's Healing and Protection Grid

- Stand in the Pillar of Light facing Archangel Uriel in the North, Archangel Rafael is in the East, Archangel Michael in the South and Archangel Gabriel in the West.
- Pull up the Red Earth Energy in two streams: one moving up your left leg, into your Root Chakra and down your right leg and one up your right leg and down your left leg back to Earth. Each is bringing up the Red Life Force of Earth and draining the pollution and dross.
- Visualize a Lavender Sphere of Light around the Four Angelic Forces above with the Legions of Yahoweh-EL emanating Lavender-pink and Magenta.
- Around the above formation, visualize an Aquamarine-Blue Bubble coming down from the heart of the Great Silent Watcher and surrounding the formation.
- Now envision the Platinum Sphere of Metatron sitting over the Bubble of the Great Silent Watcher and sealing the grid.
- Do this in the morning before you start the day and at night before you fall asleep. After each exercise, when you have completed the formation say, *"This grid will remain charged for as long as necessary until I recharge it again."*

*"I ask for the energies of Lord Melchizedek
and the thirty-three members of my Soul Lineage
to merge with me through my Five Body System.
I ask that we connect through the Cosmic Heart Chakras
over-lighted by the energies of Lord Melchizedek.
I ask that all the pain, dross and damage inflicted upon my
body, my soul and my personality aspects and those of all
Soul Lineage members, be released through this healing."*

Melchizedek

CHAPTER III

Soul Lineage of Light

Lord Melchizedek, our Universal Logos, offers us a grid to reunite us with the thirty-three members of our Soul Lineage of Light and unburden ourselves from the feeling of being alone in this world.

My Dear Hearts, I am Melchizedek.

Take a deep breath. Visualize yourself standing before Lord Melchizedek, the Universal Logos. Visualize Melchizedek in his ceremonial robe and cape of Royal Blue. In his hand is the Scepter of Universal Power and on his head, a Crown of Gold. Over his chest the Golden Cross, an Emblem of the Universal Logos, is displayed.

Visualize that Melchizedek is standing with his arms outstretched. Purple-Blue Light of the Universal Logos is emanating from the palms of his hands, Third Eye, Cosmic Heart, Personal Heart, and his Solar Plexus to you. Light is entering your entire Five Body System. It brings you the healing which removes all the pain and damage from many lifetimes of incarnation into the density of this mundane realm.

I now call forth thirty-three members of your Soul Lineage of Light. They are closely connected to your soul and aware of your Soul's Mission. They come forth to stand in a circle around you and Lord Melchizedek. They stand shoulder-to-shoulder, beaming Purple-Blue Light which is the essence and substance of Pure Melchizedek Light. Take a deep breath and make an intention for the healing that you are about to receive. Say,

"I ask for the energies of Lord Melchizedek and the thirty-three members of my Soul Lineage to merge with me through my Five Body System. I ask that we connect through the Cosmic Heart Chakras over-lighted by the energies of Lord Melchizedek. I ask that all the pain, dross and damage inflicted upon my body, my soul and my personality aspects and those of all Soul Lineage members, be released through this healing."

Take a deep breath and pause to allow the healing energies to penetrate into your Five Body System and your soul and personality aspects.

Now visualize Legions of Archangel Michael creating a circle around this entire formation. They too are standing with their shoulders touching. Their Swords of Mercy are drawn out of their sheaths and held up above the entire formation with you, Lord Melchizedek and the thirty-three members of your Soul Lineage inside the circle.

Visualize that the points of their swords touch at the center of the dome creating an electric charge of Aquamarine-Blue Light. Shimmering Aquamarine-Blue Light of Divine Mercy, Divine Protection and Divine Guidance pours down from the points of their swords into the dome, down to you. This Light will continuously charge you with energies of Divine Mercy and protect you from all lower vibrational frequencies.

Visualize that this entire formation is placed inside the Pillar of Pure White Light, brought down from the Throne of Absolute, the Abode of Divine Mother. Inside this Pillar, your energies are drawn upward to all the thrones above. Take a deep breath and pause for a moment.

We now begin the journey to ascend to each throne inside of the Pillar of Light. We reach the Throne of I Am That I Am. You stand before the Presence of I Am That I Am inside the Formation of Light with Lord Melchizedek, members of your Soul Lineage and the Angelic Forces of Michael. Visualize yourself as you merge and expand, uniting with the essence of God in Form, held within the Presence of the I Am That I Am. Take a deep breath and bathe in these energies.

We move upward inside the Pillar of Light, passing through all the Thrones in the Higher Realms until we reach to the Throne of Undifferentiated Source. This is the Throne of God in Non-Form. This is the Abode of Pure White Light. We stand before this essence in the Formation of Light with Lord Melchizedek, members of your Soul Lineage of Light and Angelic Forces of Michael. Unite, merge and receive the Light of the Undifferentiated Source. Expand in this Light, healing the pain, struggle and dross accumulated from life in physical embodiment. Now ask to be brought to the state of purity and innocence, which was originally intended for you. Say,

"I ask that all my Five Body System, mind, emotions, and my Soul's and Personality Aspects be brought back to the state of purity and innocence originally intended for me in the Divine Plan, from the heart-core of the Undifferentiated Source. I ask this on behalf of all members of my own Soul Lineage."

Take a deep breath and bathe in these energies, allow the healing to be administered to you. Together with Lord Melchizedek, the Soul Lineage members and the Angelic Forces of Michael, we travel higher and further into the depth of Light to the Throne of Absolute, the Abode of Divine Mother. We stand before the Throne of Divine Mother. Visualize that the silhouette of a female being appears from the Throne and stands before you. She may appear to you in a form of her choosing. She places her left hand on your chest and her right hand on your back, aligned with your Heart Chakra. Her Divine Light is emanating from her hands to your heart. This is the Light of the Creative Force of the Feminine Principle of Existence. This Creative Force triggers this entire creation to come into manifest form. Everything has been created from her Divine Love and Divine Grace. Through her Grace, all things are manifest and all things are possible. We shall ask her for the Original Blueprint of Perfection to be imprinted upon your body and being. Take a deep breath and pause before we receive the Blueprint.

Now say,

"I ask from the Throne of Absolute and the Presence of the Divine Mother for the Original Blueprint of the Melchizedek Light and Order to be awakened in my DNA structure and all the Fragments of my Soul to be reunited. I ask for healing,

health, and wholeness for all my Personality Aspects and Soul Fragments. I especially ask for healing of my nervous system and strength in my personality and character to help me to continue on my Soul's Divine Mission. I ask for the blessing and grace of Divine Mother to reconnect my Life Force with the Life Force of the members of my Soul Lineage, under the guidance of Lord Melchizedek, the Universal Logos. I ask to be energized, recalibrated, refreshed and reunited with the Melchizedek essence and be brought to complete health and wholeness. I ask Lord Melchizedek to over-light all my Soul Fragments and my Personality Aspects to accelerate me to fulfill my Divine Mission." Take a deep breath and visualize yourself receiving this blessing.

Now visualize that each of the Thirty-Three Members of your Soul Lineage join to overlay their own Light signature upon yours. Finally, visualize the Presence of Lord Melchizedek over-lighting your energy bodies as he sends you emanations of his Universal Light in the Presence of the Divine Mother. Health, wholeness, healing, joy, peace and harmony are restored to you from this reunion. Your Physical, Etheric, Emotional, Mental and Spiritual Bodies are refreshed, rejuvenated and overlaid by the Brilliant Light of the Universal Logos. The entire structure of your Light Body is now overlaid by the Presence of Lord Melchizedek, the Universal Logos. On your behalf, I, Melchizedek, ask and decree the following; Say,

"We ask this entire Formation of Light to continue to charge this Grid of Light with the blessings and healings which have been requested, from this day on. We ask this healing to continue and accelerate with every repetition of this meditational exercise."

Now, offer a prayer of thanksgiving to the Presence of the Divine Mother and the Throne of Absolute as we take our leave. Together with Lord Melchizedek, thirty-three members of your Soul

Lineage and the Angelic Forces of Michael we spin down through the Pillar of Light back to the Throne of the Undifferentiated Source. Offering a prayer of thanksgiving at this Throne, we continue on our downward journey to the Throne of the I Am That I Am. We offer a blessing and prayer of thanksgiving and lower our essence and energy back to the consciousness of our bodies.

Repeat this meditational exercise every day for twenty-two days and beyond. This is a great exercise to connect you with your Soul's Mission and accelerate you on your spiritual path. It will facilitate the return and reunion of all your Soul Fragments who have withdrawn their energies from you as a result of hardship and difficulties through many lifetimes in the density of Earthly Realms. A Soul Retrieval of this grand scale can bring a sense of wholeness and familiarity or belonging back to your body and being. The energies of the Universal Logos and the Melchizedek Brotherhood will support you in all your tasks and endeavors; sublime as well as mundane. Call upon the entourage of these beings to join you in dreamtime every night before you fall asleep.

With great love, I am Melchizedek. So it is.

CHAPTER IV

Sphere of Remembrance

This Grid of Light is given by St. Germain, the Master of the Seventh Ray. As the Beacons of Light and disciples of the Ascended and Living Masters, it is up to us to promote, accelerate and anchor Greater Light on Earth and pave the path for the Enlightenment of all souls and the Spiritual evolution of our planet. Use this Grid of Light with the help of St. Germain, the transmutational power of the Violet Flame, the Cosmic Power of the Lords of Light and the Creative Force of the Divine Mother, to be of greater service to our beloved Masters and to accelerate us on our own journey on the Path.

Please remember that Lord Metatron has declared the 24th of April as the celebration of Ascension Day. In a channeling session in March of 2005, Metatron said, *"I now call the 24th of April of each year the Ascension Day – Ascension Day for Earth – Ascension Day for Humanity. The 24th of April of every year will be considered Ascension Day from the Ascended Masters point of view."*

It is therefore important to celebrate this month by doing some special prayers, invocations, mantras, exercises using grids of Light and other meditational exercises, especially around the 24th.

I hold you in the Light of the Seventh Ray and the Love of St. Germain, the Lords of Light and Divine Mother.

Grid of Light with the Purple Sphere of Remembrance

My beloveds, I am St. Germain.

Visualize yourself standing in the Pillar of Light which extends above your head to the presence of the I Am That I Am and ascends up, through all the Heavenly Realms. You are standing in the presence of St. Germain. Visualize that the palms of your hands touch the palms of the hands of St. Germain. Beams of Light are emanating from my heart to your heart. These beams originate from the Purple Sphere of Remembrance in my heart. It is emanating Light from my heart to your heart. As the Light reaches you, it implodes in your heart forming the same Purple Sphere in your heart. The significance of the Purple Sphere of Remembrance is that it holds the perfect memories of your Divine Mission and the Original Blueprint for the accomplishment of your Divine Mission. The placement of this Sphere in your heart and its ignition to emit its Light to your being, allows you to recollect your Divine Mission. It will accelerate you and remove obstacles, delays and departure from your path. It will awaken your subconscious and in time your conscious recollection of your True Self and your Divine Mission on Earth.

Now say,

"I call upon the twelve members of my Council of Light to come forth."

Twelve Great Beings, who are members of your own Council of Light, come forth and take their positions in a circle around you. These are members of your Soul Lineage who have attained Mastery and ascended to Higher Realms. They are here to guide you on your path to fulfill your Divine Mission. They are gathered to give you Light and support. Visualize that the twelve council members send you Light, balancing your male and female polarities and to awakening the memories of your Divine Mission. Take a deep breath and bathe in their Light.

Now call upon your entire Soul Lineage of Light. Say,

"I call upon all members of my Soul Lineage of Light."

Visualize thirty-three members of your Soul Lineage of Light gathering in a circle around the Council of Light. These are members of your Spiritual Family of Light. Their connection with you goes beyond one lifetime. They have been with you since the beginning of time, or since the beginning of all your physical incarnations.

Visualize moving your consciousness upward inside of the Pillar of Light. We will first arrive at the Throne of the I Am That I Am.

Together, you, St. Germain, your twelve Council Members and your thirty-three Soul Lineage Members stand before the perfected Presence of the I Am That I Am, God in Form. Ask for a blessing as we merge into this Throne. Pause and take a deep breath while you bathe in the energies of the I Am That I Am. Now we move up to the Throne of YHWH. Pause and bathe in the energies of this Throne. Ask for a blessing and merge into this Throne.

Now we move our energies upward through the Pillar of Light through Realms of Reality until we reach before the Throne of Undifferentiated Source, God Beyond Form, Non-Manifest and Undifferentiated. We ask for a blessing as we merge and expand into this Throne in the entourage of our Council and Soul Lineage members who form our Grid of Light. Pause and take a deep breath in the energies of the Throne of the Undifferentiated Source.

Now we move our energies upward through the Pillar of Light to reach the Throne of Absolute and the presence of the Divine Mother. Her Feminine Creative Force holds the ideal design for all Creation in the Pool of Light which is the Throne of Creation and the Throne of Feminine Principle.

The Seven Lords of Light have their seats at the Throne of Absolute. You will come to stand before the presence of the Divine Mother in front of the Seven Lords of Light. The combined forces of all Seven Lords of Light send to us and our entourage the Aquamarine-Blue Light with Platinum shimmers, like silver dust. This is the Healing Light of the Seven Lords of Light and the Maha Lord of Light. Bathe in the energies of the Divine Mother as you receive the healing Aquamarine-Blue Platinum Light from the Lords of Light.

Pause and take a deep breath to bring greater healing and protection and to accelerate you on the path of Mastery.

Now visualize that the Angelic Forces of Yahoweh-EL, the Feminine Angelic Essence of YHWH, and Metatron are now forming around this entire formation. They stand shoulder to shoulder in a circle and begin to beam a Lavender-Pink-Purple Light to you and the members of your entourage. Pause and bathe in this healing Light.

Now visualize a Platinum Sphere of Light forming over this entire Grid of Light to seal every being and their energy inside. This will bring you protection from lower vibrations and healing from all the great beings who are invited to participate in this great Grid of Light. This Platinum Sphere will heal you, protect you and seal the higher vibrations into your body. Pause as we offer a prayer of thanksgiving to the Throne of Divine Mother and the energies of the Feminine Principle.

We now begin our descent down the Pillar of Light; first to the Throne of Undifferentiated Source, down to the Throne of YHWH and then to the Throne of I Am That I Am. We pause in each Throne to anchor the energies of the Feminine Principle and the Seven Lords of Light into each Throne and to bring the vibration of these Thrones into the consciousness of our bodies.

Hold on to the healing, the protection and the acceleration that comes to you from this entire grid formation. Use this Grid of Light daily, if you can, to accelerate the healing and to seal the energies of all aspects of your personality and fragments of your soul.

As of 20th January 2008, the entry into the Age of Aquarius and our work to bring forth the Seventh Golden Age has begun. As pioneers of this Golden Age, I ask you to call upon me, St. Germain and the Violet Ray of Transmutation, for greater healing and acceleration of your Spiritual advancement. As the Cohan of the Seventh Ray and the Guardian of the Seventh Golden Age, I am responsible for your Spiritual growth and for the evolution of this planet. I have been given the power and dispensation to heal all souls with the transmutational power of the Violet Flame and the healing power of the Violet Ray. All the Great Beings of Light are offering their help and guidance for the great feat of illuminating Earth and all Souls with Light. The Seventh Golden Age is the time for restoring order, equilibrium and facilitating our return journey to the Abode of Light. It is up to you and I to help the Light descend back to Earth and all souls.

To that end I stand by your side as your brother, St. Germain. So it is.

CHAPTER V

Power, Purity, Love, Protection and Healing

Quan Yin offers us a Grid of Light to bring forth power, purity, love, healing and protection. She also offers us a matching candle grid to accelerate and magnify the impact of the Light Grid. I chose these two grids for this month because the entire month of May is dedicated to the Divine Mother, especially Mother Mary. In both grids, Mother Mary is present with Goddess Hecate and Lady Quan Yin. Throughout the month of May, remember to invoke Mother Mary's presence and intercession in your life.

May is also the time for Wesak festival. Wesak celebrations are dedicated to Lord Buddha. Dalai Lama, the exiled spiritual and political leader of Tibet, is believed to be the 14th reincarnation of Lord Buddha.

In the Buddhist tradition, Maitreya is the expected Buddha yet to come to Earth. In the Christian Tradition, Christ is expected to return to Earth as the second coming of Christ. Christ Maitreya, the World Teacher, who is now present on Earth, represents the energies of both (for more on Christ Maitreya, go to www.share-international.org). It will be of great benefit in this month to call upon the presence of Lord Buddha and Christ Maitreya as well as Mother Mary for all personal and global intentions. Remember, on portal days, all intentions are magnified.

In this auspicious month, my prayer is that we may touch many more souls with our prayers, ceremonies and invocations and bring the awareness of the presence of the Masters to others. In this way, we will positively affect their lives and the lives of those they touch.

I wish you a happy Wesak and a great communion with the Divine Mother through these grids.

Grid of Light

My beloved Children of Light, I am Quan Yin.

I would like to give you a Grid of Light. This Grid will bring you power to better cope with your daily life. It will bring you purity to free yourself of all pain, fear, struggle, and bring you love to perform all tasks with joy. You will do this through the guardianship and guidance of Goddess Hecate, who brings you power, Goddess Quan Yin, who brings you purity, and Mother Mary, who brings you love. You will receive an Aquamarine-Blue Sphere of Protection from Archangel Michael and his Legions; a Dark-Blue Sphere of greater protection from Lord Melchizedek, our Universal Logos, and a Platinum Sphere of complete healing and protection from Lord Metatron. Both male and female Angelic Forces of EL-Shaddia and Yahoweh-EL are present.

This is a powerful and potent Grid of Light. I ask you to begin your day by visualizing this entire grid around you. Continue through the day by reminding yourself that these powerful Great Beings are around you. Copy this diagram and carry it with you. Place it where you can see it when you awaken and the last thing before you fall asleep. Place other copies in the rooms of your loved ones, in your office and in your car as a reminder to reinforce its presence and as a protection wherever you may be. Be creative and use this Grid whenever healing, protection, love, purity and power are needed.

Meditational Exercise

Visualize yourself standing at the center of a triangle (as shown in the diagram). At the three points of a triangle around you, stand Mother Mary, Lady Quan Yin and Goddess Hecate. Visualize that Mother Mary is sending you Pink Light, Quan Yin is sending you White Light and Goddess Hecate is sending you Red Light. These Lights emanate from their hearts and enter into your heart. These energies move from your heart into every cell and tissue of your body and to all your energy bodies.

Always see yourself inside of this Grid Formation. Start your day by placing yourself inside this Grid. Visualize yourself engulfed in

Pure White Light of Purity from Quan Yin, Pink Light of Divine Love from Mother Mary and the powerful, passionate Red Life Force Energy from Goddess Hecate. Know yourself to be loved, purified, and healed by these energies and brought to health and wholeness. This Grid will help you connect to the energies of the Divine Mother in three of her aspects; as Hecate for power, Quan Yin for purity and Mother Mary for love.

Around this triangle, visualize the Legions of Michael standing shoulder to shoulder. They hold their Swords of Mercy drawn out and held over your head at the center of this formation. The points of the Swords of Mercy touch and form a dome above you with Mother Mary, Quan Yin, and Hecate inside. From the touch of the points of the Swords, a beautiful Aquamarine-Blue Light begins to pour down into the dome. The Light fills the entire dome all around you and the three beings. This is the Light of Protection from Archangel Michael and his Legions. Feel yourself fully engulfed in this protective Aquamarine-Blue Light of Archangel Michael and his Legions. Take a deep breath and feel this formation around you.

Now visualize a Dark-Blue Sphere of Light around the Aquamarine-Blue Light of Archangel Michael. This shiny Dark-Blue Sphere is emanating a protective Dark-Blue Light which reflects all lower energies back to the outside world. Any negative or lower vibrational energies and any harm which may be directed at you from the outside world is transmuted at contact. No thoughts of fear, anger, depression, or aggression can penetrate through this protective sphere of Dark-Blue Light. This Sphere is offered to you by Lord Melchizedek, our Universal Logos, for your greater protection. Take a deep breath and feel the formation of the Dark-Blue Sphere of Melchizedek around you.

Now visualize that the Male and Female Aspects of the Angelic Forces of Metatron stand in a circle around the Dark-Blue Sphere of Melchizedek. The Male Aspects are known as the Angelic Forces of EL-Shaddai and the Female Aspects as the Angelic Forces of Yahoweh-EL. The forces of El-Shaddai and Yahoweh-EL are forty feet tall. They stand shoulder to shoulder holding their Rods of Power in their right hand above their heads. The tips of the rods are touching at the center of the dome directly above where you stand. When these Rods of Power are activated, a Platinum colored Light is illuminated. A shower of Platinum Light pours out from their tips.

The shower of Platinum Light from the Rods of Power forms into another Ball of Light. This is the healing and protective Platinum Sphere of Metatron. This Ball of Platinum Light is absolutely impenetrable by lower vibrations and pain. It only allows higher vibrational frequencies inside and seals you from the lower ones. Happiness, wholeness, healing, joy, peace, love and harmony are higher vibrational energies. These will be allowed in. Pain, fear and misery are stopped at contact without penetration. When someone sends you loving, kind intentions, it is allowed in and also reflected back to the person. All lower thoughts and vibrations are transmuted.

The Aquamarine-Blue Sphere of Archangel Michael and the Dark-Blue Sphere of Lord Melchizedek are the first two layers of protection. The third layer is for empowerment and is accomplished by The Angelic Forces of Yahoweh-EL and EL-Shaddai holding their Rods of Power over your head. This brings you power to accomplish your Divine Mission as well as your mundane daily chores. The last layer is the Platinum Sphere of Metatron which empowers you to receive healing, higher vibrational energies and to transmute the lower vibrations, thoughts and actions.

Every day, before you do anything, visualize this Grid of Light. It brings you healing, power, purity, protection, goodness and love. It seals that goodness inside of you and empowers you to accomplish your Divine and mundane missions.

I am your mother, Quan Yin. So it is.

Summary of Grid of Light

- Visualize yourself at the center of a triangle.
- Mother Mary, Hecate and Quan Yin stand at each point of a triangle around you.
- Mother Mary sends you Pink Light of Divine Love.
- Hecate sends you Red Light of Power and Passion.
- Quan Yin sends you White Light of Purity.
- Around the triangle, visualize Archangel Michael and his Legions standing shoulder to shoulder with their Swords of Mercy drawn out over your head. An Aquamarine-Blue Light of Protection is pouring down from the points of their swords.
- Visualize a Dark-Blue Sphere forming around the Legions of Michael. This is the Sphere of Melchizedek. It protects you from lower vibrations and seals the higher vibrations inside.
- Visualize the Angelic Forces of EL-Shaddai, the Male Angelic Aspect of Metatron, and Yahoweh-EL, the Female Angelic Aspect of Metatron standing around another circle outside of the Dark-Blue Sphere of Melchizedek. These Angelic Forces are holding their Rods of power over their heads. Platinum Light is emanating from these Rods to you.

- From the emanations of the Platinum Light, a Ball of Platinum Light forms as an outer layer around all the other formations. This is the Healing and Protective Platinum Sphere of Metatron and will absolutely seal all the higher vibrational energies inside and protect you from lower energies coming to you from outside.

Do this exercise every day as you begin your day and repeat it during the day whenever you feel your energy is lowering. Do this exercise again before you fall asleep to make your dream time a greater experience. Repeat this exercise daily for twenty two days and longer. Make a habit of setting up this grid to accelerate your healing, raise your Light vibration, heal you and keep you in pure, loving, nurturing energies and protect you from lower vibrations.

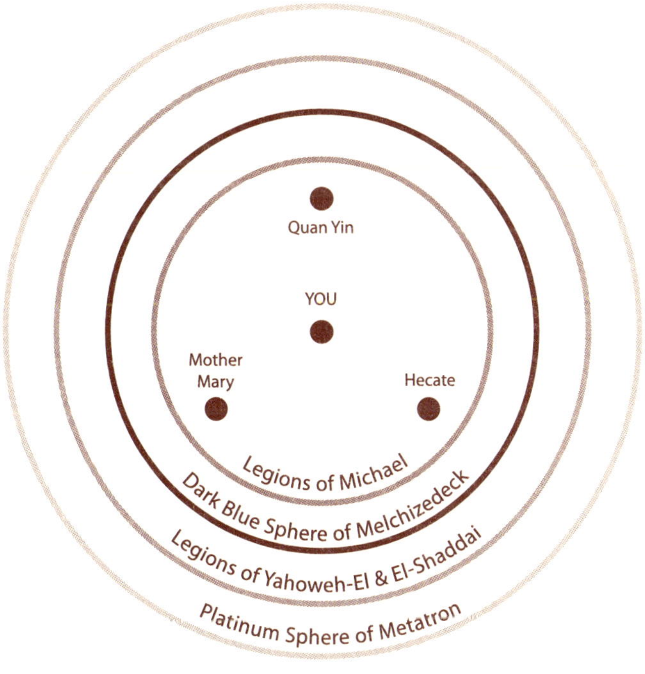

"In the name of Christ Maitreya,
I charge myself with Energies of Hope
and ask for healing of all my energy bodies
and my Five Body System."

Quan Yin

CHAPTER VI

Hope, Creativity, and Happiness

This is a Grid of Light offered by Quan Yin with an accompanying Candle Grid to add to its potency and to add momentum. Quan Yin also offers a beautiful ceremony to perform during the time of Equinox and Solstice. These are exceptionally powerful months as we begin spring and summer in the Northern Hemisphere and fall and winter in the Southern Hemisphere. Whatever we do during this time is magnified and accelerated as the portals of the Heavenly Realms are wide open.

May hope, creativity and happiness be your companions, always.

My Children of Light, I am Quan Yin.

Feel yourself comforted by your mother Quan Yin and visualize the Pure White Light of Purity and Compassion coming from my heart to yours. See yourself fully engulfed in my love.

I would like to give you a Grid of Light to clear and cleanse your energy bodies from all the dross and pain which is coming to the surface from Earth's natural disasters, war and unrest throughout the world. Please understand that this is part of the process of cleansing for Earth. The Masters are watching over all of you. Those of you working in service to the Light may feel the weight of this dross more dramatically than the unconscious masses. I bring this Grid of Light to help you boost your energy fields and feel greater hope, creativity and happiness in your lives.

I offer you a Candle Grid to magnify the impact of the Grid of Light. It is best to do them both together as each will magnify the impact of the other. Finally, I bring you a ceremony to anchor and magnify these energies on Earth.

This exercise is timely because of the upcoming Solstice. As you practice the Grid of Light you will begin to gain momentum. It is therefore best to begin exercising the Grid of Light during the Summer Solstice (June 19-22) and during the ten-day phase around the Solstice (from June 15 to 25). The gateways of the Heavenly Realms are wide open the day of, the day before, and the day after each Solstice and Equinox which is the time of the changing of the seasons. These are moments in time when your spiritual exercises can be magnified and the impact accelerated.

Grid of Light for Hope, Creativity and Happiness

Take a deep breath and visualize yourself standing at the center of a triangle. The points of the triangle are in the North, Southeast, and Southwest.

Visualize yourself facing the North point of the triangle. Christ Maitreya is standing at that North point facing you. He is standing inside a Pillar of Bright Emerald-Green Light. This is the Pillar of Hope. Focus your energy at his presence and step into the pillar of Emerald-Green Light. Take a deep breath and merge into the presence of Christ Maitreya. Bathe in his presence and allow yourself to be filled with Energies of Hope. Now say,

"In the name of Christ Maitreya, I charge myself with Energies of Hope and ask for healing of all my energy bodies and my Five Body System." Pause and take a deep breath.

Return to your position at the center of the triangle. Now turn and face the next point of the triangle in the Southeast. Place your focus on the Pillar of Bright Orange Light. This is the Pillar of Creativity. Archangel Ariel, the Angel of Creativity, is standing inside this Pillar of Light. Bright Orange Light is emanating from this Archangel's body. Take a deep breath and visualize yourself stepping inside this Pillar of Light. Bathe in the refreshing and energizing Creative Force of this Archangel and the Creative Force of Nature. Now say,

"In the name of Archangel Ariel, I charge myself with the Energies of Creativity and ask for healing of all my energy bodies and my Five Body System." Pause and take a deep breath.

Step out of the Southeast point and return to your position at the center. Now turn and face the next point of the triangle in the Southwest. Now place your focus on the Pillar of Bright White Light. This is the Pillar of Happiness. Quan Yin is standing at this point inside the Pillar. Visualize yourself stepping into this Pillar. Bathe in the Bright White Light of Happiness and Compassion emanating from Quan Yin. Now say,

"In the name of Quan Yin, I charge myself with the Energies of Happiness and Compassion and ask for healing of all my energy bodies and my Five Body System." Take a deep breath and pause for a moment.

Return to the center facing the North point of the triangle. Visualize that the three pillars begin to expand and enlarge to reach and merge into each other with you at the center. The Green Pillar of Hope, the Orange Pillar of Creativity, and the White Pillar of Happiness extend, expand, and overlap into each other to create one large Pillar of Light that encompasses the entire triangle, forming a huge circle.

From the merging of the three Pillars of Light, streams of Peach and Citron-Green Light begin to emanate in every direction inside the circle. This is the Pure Essence of the Feminine and Masculine Energies for the Seventh Golden Age. The Peach represents the Pure and Innocent Female Child and the Citron-Green represents the Clear and Focused Energies of the Male Child. These Energies will restore us to the perfection of the Original Divine Plan intended for humankind. This is what the Masters have been working to attain, on behalf of humankind and through the help of you who are in service to the Masters of Light.

Bathe in the streams of Peach and Citron-Green Light and experience the United Force of Hope, Creativity and Happiness merge into every cell, every molecule, and every iota of your bodies and being. Take a deep breath and pause for a moment. Now say,

"In the name of Divine Mother in all of her aspects, I ask for the Energies of Hope, Creativity and Happiness to remain with me all the time. I invite Christ

Maitreya, Ariel and Quan Yin to energize my Five Body System with their Light and their presence from this day on. This Grid of Light will continue to remain charged and will gain momentum and acceleration with each repetition."

Take a deep breath and feel yourself engulfed with the Peach-Citron Energies. Remind yourself that the energies of Hope, Creativity and Happiness are surrounding you at all times.

Use the Grid of Light anywhere, at any time, as many times as you can.

Quan Yin's Grid of Light
for Hope, Creativity and Happiness

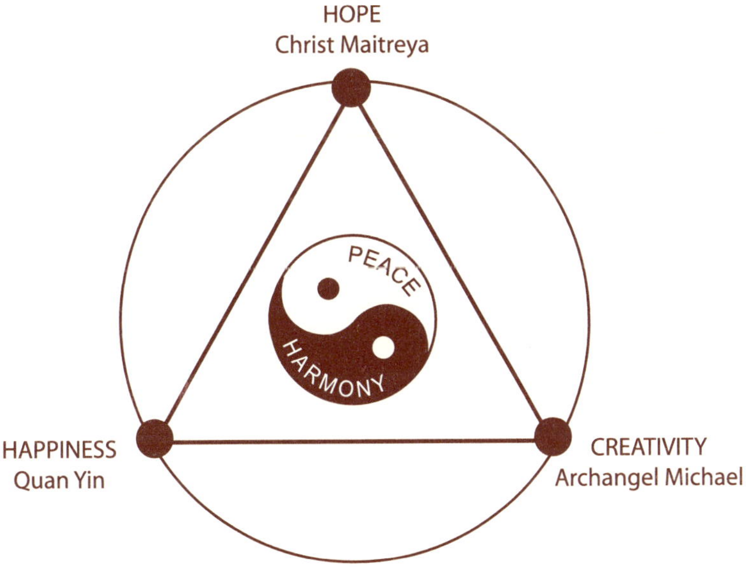

Candle Grid for Hope, Creativity and Happiness

You may use this candle grid for any length of time. Lighting the candle grid for an entire month will bring the best results. The ten-day period around the Solstice will have the height of magnification of all energies. Keep your candle grid lit for a longer time when possible during this time. This will magnify the impact of the grid of Light exercise and your healing. It will be beautiful to light the candle grid before you perform the healing exercise.

Materials Needed

- White poster board
- Purple or blue felt-tip pen
- Cinnamon
- Candles: Three pillar candles (3"x 9" or 2"x 6" pillars) or 3 votive candles which you can replace as they run out. For the grid, you can use a green candle for Hope, an orange candle for Creativity, and a white candle for Happiness and Compassion. To simplify you can use all white candles, as each candle will be charged with the energies of Hope, Creativity and Happiness. The color is not of great significance.

Instructions to Create Your Grid

Duplicate the diagram as shown or follow these instructions:

- Cut the poster board so it becomes a square.
- Draw a circle on the square poster board. (use a big plate or round tray as a guide)

- Draw an equilateral triangle inside the circle so the North, Southeast and Southwest points of the triangle touch the circle.
- Inside the triangle draw a circle 2 inches in diameter. Inside of this circle draw the sign of yin yang. On the upper portion of the yin-yang sign, write the word, *"Peace."* On the lower portion of the yin-yang sign, write the word, *"Harmony."*
- At the North point of the triangle write, *"Hope"* and *"Christ Maitreya."*
- At the Southeast point of the triangle write, *"Creativity"* and *"Archangel Ariel."*
- At the Southwest point of the triangle write, *"Happiness"* and *"Quan Yin."*
- Place a mound of cinnamon on the yin-yang sign.
- Sprinkle cinnamon along the entire circumference of the large outermost circle.
- Place the green (or white) candle at the North point on top of the words *"Hope"* and *"Christ Maitreya."*
- Place the orange (or white) candle at the Southeast point on top of the words *"Creativity"* and *"Archangel Ariel."*
- Place the white candle at the Southwest point on top of the words *"Happiness"* and *"Quan Yin."*

Charging your Candle Grid for the First Time

- Pick up the green (or white) Candle of Hope at the North point, hold it both hands, raise it above your head and say,

  "In the name of Christ Maitreya, I charge this candle with Energies of Hope and ask for healing of all my Energy Bodies and my Five Body System."

- Place this candle back in its position on the Grid.
- Pick up the Orange (or white) Candle of Creativity in the Southeast point, hold it both hands, raise it above your head and say,

  "In the name of Archangel Ariel, I charge this candle with the Energies of Creativity and ask for healing of all my Energy Bodies and my Five Body System."

- Place this candle back in its position on the Grid.
- Pick up the White Candle of Happiness in the Southwest point, hold it both hands, raise it above your head and say,

  "In the name of Quan Yin, I charge this candle with the Energies of Happiness and Compassion and ask for healing of all my Energy Bodies and my Five Body System."

- Place this candle back in its position on the Grid.

Lighting the Candles

- First light the green Candle of Hope and say,

  "I light this Flame of Hope in the name of Christ Maitreya and ask for the Energies of Hope to fill my life and my Being."

- Then light the orange Candle of Creativity and say,

  "I light this Flame of Creativity in the name of Archangel Ariel and ask for the Energies of Creativity to fill my life and my Being."

- Then light the white Candle of Happiness and say,

  "I light this Flame of Happiness in the name of Quan Yin and ask for the Energies of Happiness and Compassion to fill my life and my Being."

Now the Grid is completely charged. From this point on, each time you light the Grid simply say the invocations above for each of the candles.

Ceremony of Hope, Creativity and Happiness for the Summer Solstice

I offer you two ways to do this ceremony, alone or as a group of four. Find out when the Solstice occurs during your time zone and perform this ceremony at least once during the seventy two hour period, on the day of the Solstice, the day before and the day after. It will be even more potent to perform this ceremony daily during the ten days before, during and after the Solstice, in the months of June and December and during the Equinoxes, in the months of March and September. You may perform this ceremony at any other time of the year that you feel drawn, as it brings great Blessings and Light to you, the Earth and all humankind.

This ceremony can be performed inside or outside in the open. If you do it inside, visualize that the circle and triangle are drawn around you. When you have completed the ceremony, remember to remove and clear the Grid by invoking the Violet Flame. Do this by saying,

"I invoke the Violet Flame of Transmutation to encapsulate this ceremonial site, keeping it undisturbed by any external sources." In this way the Energy of the Grid will remain active at that location, undisturbed and unaffected by any later activity on that site.

If you perform it outside, you can draw the circle, the triangle, and the small yin-yang circle on the sand or on the ground. When you have completed the ceremony, remember to remove and clear the markings from the ground. Do this by rubbing or wiping them away and, if water is available, pour some water over it to clear and remove the Grid. Then say the Violet Flame invocation,

"I invoke the Violet Flame of Transmutation to encapsulate this ceremonial site, keeping it undisturbed by any external sources."

In this way the Energy of the Grid will remain active at that location, undisturbed and unaffected by any later activity on that site.

Ceremony for One Person

Performing this ceremony each day during the times of the Equinox and Solstice is of great benefit as each repetition adds momentum to the whole. To do it on your own, you will need four crystals. The crystals will be placed on each of the three points of the triangle and in the center. The size and type of crystal is entirely up to you as you will be charging them with the relevant energy according to their placement at each point.

- To start the ceremony, stand outside of the Grid, take a deep breath and center yourself by visualizing you are inside the Pillar of Light. You are connected to the Heavenly Realms through your Crown Chakra and to the Earthly Realms through the bottoms of your feet and your Earth Crust Chakra.

- Say a prayer to ask for a blessing and connect to the Energies of Mother Earth below you and to the Divine Mother above you,

  "I invoke the presence of the Divine Mother in her Heavenly and Earthly Aspects. I connect myself to the Energies of the Divine Mother bringing the Heavenly Realms to the Earth and anchoring those Energies through my body into the Earth. I connect to the energies of the Earthly Realms by pulling the Life Force from the heart core of Mother Earth into my Earth Crust Chakra and to my body, through my feet. I call upon Goddess Gaia, the Deity of Earth to supervise and implement this action. I call upon the presence of Christ Maitreya, Archangel Ariel and Quan Yin to bring the Energies of Hope, Creativity and Happiness and to bless and facilitate this ceremony." Take a deep breath and pause for a moment to gather the energies.

- Step into the position of North, facing the center of the triangle and say,

  "I now charge myself with the Energy of Hope and I ask Christ Maitreya to embody me." Pause, take a deep breath and anchor the Energies in that position.

- Move to the direction of Southeast. Face the center of the triangle and say,

  "I now charge myself with the Energy of Creativity and I ask Archangel Ariel to embody me." Pause and take a deep breath and anchor the Energies in that position.

- Move to the direction of Southwest. Face the center of the triangle and say,

  "I now charge myself with the Energy of Happiness and I ask Quan Yin to embody me." Pause and take a deep breath and anchor the Energies in that position.

- Now move to the center of the triangle. Stand in the center and say,

  "I now charge myself with the Energy of Peach Light, the Light of the Pure and Innocent Female Child, the Citron-Green Light of the Clear and Focused Male Child, and I ask Divine Mother to embody me." Pause and take a deep breath and anchor the Energies in that position.

- The ceremony is complete at this point. When you are complete, leave the circle. Remember to remove and clear the Grid by invoking the Violet Flame. Do this by saying,

  "I invoke the Violet Flame of Transmutation to encapsulate this ceremonial site, keeping it undisturbed by any external sources."

In this way the Energy of the Grid will remain active at that location, undisturbed and unaffected by any later activity on that site.

Ceremony for Four People

Ideally you would perform this ceremony, with a total of four people, outdoors to bless Nature and Mother Earth. You may also perform it indoors. Wherever you do it, the environment will be blessed.

- First, all four people will stand outside the perimeter of the formation and say the following invocation out loud to ask for a blessing and connect to the Energies of Mother Earth below and to the Divine Mother above,

"I invoke the presence of the Divine Mother in her Heavenly and Earthly Aspects. I connect myself to the Energies of the Divine Mother bringing the Heavenly Realms to the Earth and anchoring those Energies through my body into the Earth. I call upon the presence of Christ Maitreya, Archangel Ariel and Quan Yin to bring the Energies of Hope, Creativity and Happiness and to bless and facilitate this ceremony."

- Then each person enters inside the Grid, choosing to stand in one of the points of the triangle or in the center. The person in the center faces north and the people at the points of the triangle face the center.
- When everyone has taken their position, begin the invocations. Starting at the north point, the person standing in that position says aloud,

  "I now charge myself with the Energy of Hope and I ask Christ Maitreya to embody me." Now pause, take a deep breath and anchor the Energies in that position.
- Then, raise your arms with the palms of each hand facing the center of the triangle, and send the Energies of Hope and the blessing of Christ Maitreya to the person in the center.
- Next, the person standing in the Southeast says,

  "I now charge myself with the Energy of Creativity and I ask Archangel Ariel to embody me."
- Pause and take a deep breath and anchor the Energies in that position. Then, raise your arms with the palms

of each hand facing the center of the triangle, and send the Energies of Creativity and the blessing of Archangel Ariel to the person in the center.

- Next the person standing in the Southwest says,

  "I now charge myself with the Energy of Happiness and I ask Quan Yin to embody me."

- Pause and take a deep breath and anchor the Energies in that position. Then raise your arms with the palms of each hand facing the center of the triangle and send the Energies of Happiness and the blessings of Quan Yin to the person in the center.

- The person standing in the Center says,

  "I now charge myself with the Energies of Peach and Citron-Green Light representing the Light of the Pure and Innocent Female Child and the Clear and Focused Male Child, and I ask Divine Mother to embody me."

- The person in the center now receives energies from the Heavenly Realms and transmits them to Earth. This is done by raising their right arm high above their head, pointing the fingers of the right hand straight up to receive the Divine Mother Energies from the Heavens above. At the same time, the left arm and fingers are pointing downward to the Earth below to transmit the Heavenly Divine Mother Energies to bless Mother Earth.

- After the recitation of all the invocations and while the hands are still in position, pause for a moment, take a deep breath, and fully bathe in all the Energies.

- The ceremony is complete at this point and everyone lowers their arms and leaves the grid.
- When you have completed the ceremony, remember to remove and clear the grid by invoking the Violet Flame. Do this by saying,

  "I invoke the Violet Flame of Transmutation to encapsulate this ceremonial site, keeping it undisturbed by any external sources."

  In this way the Energy of the Grid will remain active at that location, undisturbed and unaffected by any later activity on that site.

To gather momentum, do this ceremony four times by rotating each person into each of the four positions and repeating the instructions. In this way, each person has the chance to anchor and receive the Energies at all four points of the Grid. This is done by moving clockwise. Center moves to North. North moves to Southeast. Southeast moves to Southwest. Southwest moves to the Center.

I am your mother, Quan Yin. So it is.

"The Flame of God-Unity is the spark of Divine Light which connects you to the Undifferentiated Source."

Master Thoth

CHAPTER VII

Empowerment and Purity

Sanat Kumara offers us a meditational journey to visit with Master Thoth and receive the Emerald-Green Light of Empowerment and Healing. Sanat Kumara also presents us with the Lavender Light of the Feminine Creative Force. This meditational exercise is intended to release all impurities from our bodies, our environment and our planet.

I wish you a wonderful and happy journey with Sanat Kumara and Master Thoth.

Thoth's Emerald-Green Light of Empowerment and Sanat Kumara's Lavender Light of Purity

Beloveds, I am Sanat Kumara.

To begin, I will place a Bubble of Protection and Focus around you to prevent you from being distracted. Take a deep breath and focus your energies on your Third Eye.

Visualize yourself standing inside this Bubble of Light. Archangel Uriel, Archangel Raphael, Archangel Michael, and Archangel Gabriel are standing around you in the four directions. Uriel is in the North, Raphael in the East, Michael in the South and Gabriel in the West. Each of the Angelic Forces is sending you Light from their own energetic force field. Yellow Light is beamed to you from Uriel, Pink from Raphael, Aquamarine-Blue from Michael and Green from Gabriel. Pause and bathe in the Energies of these Angelic Forces. Take a deep breath.

I now call upon Master Thoth, the Master Alchemist, to come forth. Visualize him approaching to stand in front of you. He is forty feet tall. An emblem made of sacred geometric shapes is illuminated over his Personal Heart Chakra. Focus on this emblem. Geometric shapes are illuminated in Emerald-Green colors. At the center of these geometries, symbols begin to form. The symbols look like the fire letters of Hebrew or the sacred letters of Sanskrit. Notice that these are multi-layered geometries. Pause and see the fire letters fully form inside the multi-layered geometries. All are vibrating Emerald-Green Light. Take a deep breath and bathe in the healing Emerald-Green Light.

The Emerald-Green Light becomes brighter in the center until it turns to White Light, pushing the Emerald-Green to the edges. These beams of Emerald-Green Light expand to create a Bubble around you and the four Angelic Forces. Bathe for a moment in these Energies. While you continue to bathe in the Emerald-Green Light, I will talk about Master Thoth. At this present juncture in Earth's history, Master Thoth is pulling major alchemical powers to change the course of events. Metatron, St Germain and I have talked at different times regarding Alchemy. It is applied when you turn something; some object or some energy, from a lower energy field, from a lower level of existence, to a higher one. Magic is applied when you materialize or manifest something out of nothing. This refers to materializing an object entirely "from thin air."

Both Alchemy and Magic work with the Five Elements which are the building blocks for the creation of this manifest reality. Magic works with the elements of Air and Ether. Alchemy works with the more dense elements of Fire, Earth and Water. With these three Elements, an Alchemist changes the nature of something that is already in existence, thereby moving the energy of that thing or event from a lower vibration to a higher one. The process, as the famous saying goes, changes "base metal into gold."

Master Thoth is capable of administering both Alchemical reaction and Magic, which is the materialization of an object "from thin air." In the process of our work together, and in what I am about to teach you, we need to achieve both. First we need to change the alchemical nature of all events and then bring in new events, through the magic of instant manifestation. These are brought from the non-material realms to the material realms of this third dimensional reality. Then, to adjust and arrange time and space in such a way that the new events will fit perfectly, from the Non-Manifest Realm into the Manifest Realm. At that point, we would achieve the Alchemy of changing base metal into gold and the Magic of the Non-Manifest brought to Manifest.

In this meditational exercise, you will visit Master Thoth. He will work with you to change the alchemy of the base metal of events into gold. He will teach you to change the Alchemy of your disempowerment, fears, and concerns, to the Gold of Empowerment, Power and Might. The empowerment will be reached when you learn the Alchemy of pulling the forces of Power and Might to yourself.

Empowerment Meditation with Master Thoth

Bring your attention to the Grid of Light for protection and focus around you. Become aware that you are standing at the center of a circle. Archangels Uriel, Raphael, Michael and Gabriel, are sending you beams of Light in the colors of Yellow, Pink, Aquamarine-Blue and Green. Master Thoth is beaming his own Emerald-Green Light from his heart to you and the four Angelic Forces around you. Inside the beams of Light, the sacred geometries are pouring forth. The Emerald-Green Bubble of Master Thoth's Energy is fully formed around you.

Focus on the Sacred Geometries emanating from the Emblem on Master Thoth's chest. Something in the Sacred Geometry will pull you to itself. Focus on the Sacred Geometries and the Fire Letters and let the one that needs to energize and commune with you, magnetize you to itself. When it magnetizes your energy field to itself, go with it and let it pull you in. You will go through a Portal of Light. You have now reached the inner sanctum of Master Thoth's heart. Take a moment and bathe in these energies. Take a deep breath.

Adonai beloveds, I am Thoth.

In the Sacred Space of the Inner Chamber of my own Heart, I offer you my Healing Light. In the space of your Personal Heart I place a Sacred Geometry. This Sacred Emblem is emanating from my own Heart Chakra. I will take this emblem into the palm of my left hand and place it in the center of your Heart Chakra. The Sacred Geometry which you receive will bring healing and balance to your Male and Female Polarities. It will also enhance your connection with me. Receive this as I place it directly over the Flame of God-Unity in the center of your Personal Heart Chakra. The Flame of God-Unity is the spark of Divine Light which connects you to The Undifferentiated Source.

The Sacred Geometry, which I place over the Flame of God-Unity in your heart, is to empower and accelerate you to pull to yourself events that fulfill all your needs, including the needs of your body, mind, emotions, soul and spirit. It will also help you fulfill your Soul's Mission and those commitments requested of you by the Masters such as Ancient of Days, Melchizedek, Sanat Kumara and Christ Maitreya, as well as your own Guides. Power and Might is embedded in the Sacred Geometries. By repeating this meditational exercise, you will gain momentum in achieving greater power and might to attain your Divine Mission and to attain success in the mundane.

We all work to return from the depth of darkness to the Light of Creation and the Energies of the Feminine Principle. It therefore goes without saying that every one of the Masters is fully aligned with the Will of the Feminine Principle and the Energies of the Divine Mother. The Divine Mother has retrieved your Soul Mission from the Pool of Creation. She has chosen the path according to what is of greatest service and how your own energy can be expanded to provide that service. I will personally see to it that all the alchemical processes are in place for you to accomplish this mission. The Sacred Geometry is now forming over your Personal Heart. Take a deep breath.

I will now describe the two components of the Sacred Geometry. There are Male and Female Polarities to this Sacred Geometry. The Sacred Geometry in its Male or Electronic Polarity manifests as a large Truncated Sphere of Light which is spinning around its center creating an Electronic Force Field. This Truncated Sphere is a dodecahedron, similar to a soccer ball made of Emerald-Green Light. The Female Polarity is a Golden Seed. The Feminine component sits at the center, superimposed, over the Flame of God-Unity and creates a Magnetic Force Field.

The large Truncated Sphere begins to spin and gain momentum until it implodes into the Magnetic Force Field of the Seed causing it to explode outward. The explosion goes outward forming the shape of a Rose Bud. Rose Petals begin to open up as it expands outward. The rose is symbolic of the Creative Force. It represents the Manifest Form of the Divine Feminine. When it goes back to non-manifest it becomes a seed which looks like a brain. All compartments of the brain are folded in. This brain-like geometry is deeply hidden in the center core of the Rose Bud.

Visualize the Truncated Sphere spinning around the Seed in the center. Both gain momentum until the large Truncated Sphere is pulled to the center, causing an implosion. The geometric shape in the center begins to expand after the implosion to become an explosion. Take a deep breath and pause while you visualize the force of implode - explode continuing for five times.

I offer you my love and my support. I ask you to call upon Thoth to work with you at night. I will work with you on the Alchemy of Time and Space; to bring you Power and Might to achieve all that you have agreed and intended to achieve in both the mundane realms and the sublime on behalf of your Soul, your Soul Lineage, the Masters and your Personality Aspects. This will accelerate your success. Every night call upon me and say,

"I call upon Master Thoth to reactivate and recalibrate me to the highest of my Soul and Personality's potential, my highest potential. Bring me the Power and Might to express the Alchemy of turning base metal into gold through my being, to manifest the sublime in the mundane and achieve my highest Divine Mission on behalf of my Soul, my Soul Lineage and the Masters."

I hold you with great love in my own heart. I thank you and I look forward to our work and our communion.

I am Thoth. So it is.

The Lavender Platinum Light of the Feminine Child

Sanat Kumara resumes.

Beloveds, be mindful of the energy of Platinum Light mixed with Lavender. This Lavender colored Light represents the Feminine Child, the Daughter Aspect in the Trinity of the New Age. Metatron has been working on this for the past decade. This is a process which utilizes alchemy. The alchemy of the Aquamarine-Blue and Citron colored Light of the Masculine Principle for the New Age is merging with the Peach-Pink colored Light of the Feminine Principle, to bring the New Age into a state of birthing. The Child Aspect, which in this case is a Feminine Child, is represented in Lavender or Lilac colored Light. To give it Power and Might for full manifestation, the Divine Mother adds her Platinum colored Light. It becomes manifest in Lavender-Lilac Light with Platinum Shimmers, representing the Pure and Innocent Feminine Child.

Many varieties of amethyst, especially amethyst geodes, represent, enhance and accelerate this process. Amethyst will be one of our most important gem stones for the anchoring of the energies of the Pure and Innocent Female Child Aspect. It is important to obtain and charge the individual pieces by calling upon the Energies of the Feminine Principle, the Masculine Principle and the Pure and Innocent Feminine Child for the New Golden Age. The geodes have the advantage of representing both the womb and the newly born child.

I invite the presence of Christ Maitreya, the Elohim, Lord Melchizedek, Ancient of Days, the Twenty-Four Elders, the Seven Kumaras, Thoth, Metatron and the Divine Mother. I ask you to visualize that everyone is standing around a circle, including yourself and Sanat

Kumara. In the center, visualize the Globe of Planet Earth. Imagine that everyone is holding their arms up with hands facing the Globe. From the palms of everyone's hands and from the center of the heart, beams of Lavender-Lilac Light are emanating.

The Divine Mother in all of her Aspects as all the Female Goddesses and Deities and Metatron, in all of Metatron's Aspects, as EL-Shaddai, YHWH, Yahoweh-EL, are creating Beams of Platinum Light from their hearts and their hands. This Platinum Light is suspended in the air in the form of shimmers that fall from above and reach all around. We all send Lavender from our palms and our heart. The members of the Seven Hierarchies, (the Ancient of Days, the Melchizedeks, Thoths, Metatrons, Elohim, Kumaras, and Christ Maitreya) form a circle around you. Take a deep breath.

We invite the Brotherhood of the White Lodge to come forth and become part of this circle around the Globe. For every person, Master, Great Being, God, Goddess and Deity who wishes to join us in this circle, we invite the Seven Hierarchies to create an individual circle. In this manner the numbers increase and multiply and the impact intensifies. Everyone around the circle is beaming Lilac Light to the Globe. From above, below and in every direction Metatron and the Divine Mother send the Platinum Shimmering Light.

Now we call the Seven Lords of Light to create a circle around you and the Seven Hierarchies. Around these two circles we call the Maha Lord of Light to create a third circle. We have now created a huge circle around the globe made up of you and multitudes of Great Beings of Light. Each Being is encircled by three rings made up of the Seven Hierarchies, the Seven Lords of Light and the Maha Lord of Light. Take a deep breath and pause to establish this image in your mind's eye.

Train your mind to make this Grid of Light as an ongoing exercise. Keep visualizing the Lilac colored Light emanating to Earth and the shimmering Platinum Light dropping like rain drops onto Earth; then mixing and merging and being absorbed by Earth like dew drops on a thirsty plant; like drops of nectar, rain drops of Love or dew drops of Platinum.

Through this exercise, the Light of the Masters who work with you on this project will become stronger. We have brought this pregnancy to this point. The present state of Earth's evolution is like labor pains. At this point in Earth's evolution and the spiritual evolution of the masses, we are faced with a great re-birthing phenomenon. Indeed we are all watching very carefully to make sure that the labor pangs will bear the fruit of the birthing of the Pure and Innocent Feminine Child, the Daughter Principle. This is why the Divine Mother asks you to pray for her. Take a deep breath.

I hold you in my own heart. I am well pleased the work that we accomplish together.

I am Sanat Kumara. So it is.

CHAPTER VIII

Sphere of Illumination and Flame of God-Unity

In this exercise, St. Germain begins by illuminating the Flame of God-Unity inside the Sphere of Remembrance within our Heart Chakras. Then, clad in our Ceremonial Robes, St. Germain leads us to the Thrones of God. At the Throne of the I Am That I Am, we receive the blessing of Sanat Kumara and are joined by Archangel Uriel to form a Grid of Light. We continue in this Grid of Light on our journey to visit the higher Thrones. Once we reach the Throne of Absolute, we kneel before the presence of our beloved Divine Mother and ask her to intercede on our behalf and help us to become the instrument of change and the conduit for receiving the Blueprint for Perfection as was intended for us in the Original Divine Plan.

St. Germain further beckons us to seek financial means, power, prosperity and unlimited supply of abundance in order to serve the Light and facilitate the presence of the energies of Divine Mother and the Masters of Light on Earth. The Seven Mighty Elohim, EL-Shaddai, Yahoweh-EL, Ancient of Days and the Great Silent Watcher are called to add further valor to our intentions.

My beloveds, I am St. Germain.

I would like to ask you to light a purple candle at all times when you are in your house. Call upon St. Germain to energize it for you. You may keep it lit during the night while you sleep as long as it does not cause a fire hazard. You may place it inside a cup or ceramic jar both for safety and protection from fire and to dim the bright Light. Place it close to you and no more than three to four feet away. The Purple Light can transmute all the dross and awaken your energy centers. It will accelerate you in opening up to the higher energies.

Take a deep breath and focus your energy in the center of your chest. Feel the presence of St. Germain by your side. Visualize that you are facing St. Germain. I am in my Ceremonial Robes. Around my shoulders I wear a Purple Cape. In my right hand I hold a Purple Scepter; on my head is a Gold Crown with a Purple Gem which sits right over my Third Eye.

You wear your own Purple Cape. Your Scepter has emeralds, rubies and sapphires. A Scepter is the symbol for power and authority. The gem on your crown is a Deep Purple-Blue Sapphire. Your crown is large and wide. You can feel its weight on top of your head. You can also feel a cool energy from the Sapphire directly over your Third Eye. The cool energy of the gold covers the back of your neck and sits over your Channeling Chakra. The Crown connects these two energy centers; the Third Eye on your forehead and the Fourth Eye at the back of your neck. To give you an idea of the exact location of the Fourth Eye, imagine an imaginary line going diagonally through the Third Eye to come out exactly where your head sits over the neck. That is your Channeling Chakra. The Third Eye is the center for Inner Visual Perception and the Channeling Chakra, or the Fourth Eye at the back of the neck, is the center for Inner Verbal Communication.

Through these two chakras you hear the guiding voice and experience the visual perception from the Masters of the Inner Realms. This you already experience in dream time. Once activated, you will be able to experience it in waking consciousness at day and at night.

Visualize that St. Germain is now placing his left hand over your Heart Chakra. Feel the warmth moving from my hand into your Heart Chakra. Focus on this area and imagine a Sphere of Purple Light begin to form in the center of your Heart Chakra. In the center of this Sphere, a Golden-Yellow Flame is lit. This is the Flame of God-Unity. The Purple Sphere is the Sphere of Remembrance. Its task is to emanate the Light of remembrance to your Heart Chakra. From your Heart Chakra, the Light emanates to all your Five Body System. The memory of yourself in Oneness with the Source of Creation is held within this Sphere. This memory has been lost over many lifetimes of incarnations in the density of this Mundane Realm of Matter. The presence of the Sphere of Remembrance brings back the memories of that Oneness to you. It allows you to recall that Oneness back to yourself. The experience of separation and loneliness will leave you once this Sphere is fully established in your Heart Chakra.

The Sphere of Remembrance, once fully illuminated, becomes the Sphere of Illumination. It will retrieve the memories, patterns, designs, thought forms and actions from the mind of God, the Undifferentiated Source. These will unfold and manifest in this third dimensional reality as actions which lead you to your Divine Mission and illuminate the path to reach Enlightenment.

Feel the warmth from the hand of St. Germain as I beam the Light of Remembrance to the Sphere in your Heart Chakra at the center of your chest. The Sphere of Remembrance is Purple outside and Golden-Yellow inside. The Flame of God-Unity is the source of Oneness with all people, places and things. Everything is in Oneness with the Universal Consciousness of God or "All That Is." All that I am is held within this Flame. All that you are is held within this Flame. The Inner Flame illuminates the thought forms for ideas, designs and concepts which turn into actions once the entire Sphere is activated. Visualize that the Flame is becoming brighter and larger until it explodes into the entire Sphere. The Purple color of the Sphere and the Golden-Yellow color of the Flame merge to create a Peach-Pink Light. The Sphere implodes inside your Heart Chakra to release knowledge, wisdom and information into your Heart Chakra. The Sphere of Remembrance is now fully activated and illuminated. At this stage, it becomes the Sphere of Illumination.

This Sphere will illuminate your Heart Chakra and your Five Body System with the Pure White Light held within the heart of the Undifferentiated Source. Ideas, designs and concepts can now be retrieved from the heart of the Undifferentiated Source to be turned into action through you.

Now, visualize that the Pillar of Light begins to form around us to connect us to the Higher Realms. Inside of this Pillar of Light, you and I will merge into Oneness. We will move up inside of the Pillar of Light to the Thrones. Envision that we reach the Throne of I Am That I Am, God in Form. Your own perfected presence of the I Am resides here. As we stand before the Throne, notice that Sanat Kumara, the Planetary Logos for Earth is present. Uniting and merging with Sanat Kumara will help the energies of the Planetary Logos be anchored on Earth through you. This will help the planet and the consciousness of all souls. This union will also help you to retrieve ideas and designs from the Universal Consciousness of the Planetary Logos. Sanat Kumara's consciousness is over-lighting the entire body of this planet and the consciousness of all souls, even though for the most part, the consciousness of all souls is asleep to his presence. His presence is holding together the consciousness of every soul, sentient, non-sentient, mineral, animal and human. All people, places and things are held in his consciousness.

At the Throne of the I Am That I Am, we merge into the consciousness of Sanat Kumara. We ask him to over-light our bodies and allow him to use our bodies to over-light Earth to anchor his energies, essence, physical embodiment and his beingness on Earth. Archangel Uriel joins us and merges into the presence with us. Now visualize that you stand in the North and St. Germain stands in the

South, Sanat Kumara in the East and Archangel Uriel in the West. At the center is the Throne of the I Am That I Am.

The four make a diamond shaped portal and begin to spin. The spin will pull the four energies into the center to implode into the Throne of the I Am That I Am.

Visualize this formation imploding into your Heart Chakra and exploding out. Beams of Light emanate in every direction. The implosion-explosion sequence becomes faster inside of the Pillar of Light. Pause and take a deep breath.

We spiral up to the Throne of YHWH in the twenty-second Realm. The Throne of YHWH is a Golden Throne and the seat is emanating Pure Golden Light Energies.

We will form a circle around the Throne of YHWH. You, St. Germain, Sanat Kumara and Archangel Uriel together with the energies of the Presence of the I Am which have accompanied us to this Throne. Once again the energy of The Seat of the Throne will begin to pulse and pull everyone into it. We begin to spin around. The spin becomes faster. We are pulled into the Throne of YHWH and implode. The Liquid Golden Light Energy of the Throne begins to vibrate through us in every which direction exploding and imploding. With each explosion and implosion the Light increases and the power extends. We gain outward momentum and begin to ascend inside the Pillar of Light to the Throne of God-Source.

Moving up, we spiral to reach the Throne of God-Source, at the thirty-third Realm. Cobalt-Blue Light of the Throne showers upon us. We stand around the Throne in our formation of the Grid of Light with Sanat Kumara, Uriel, you and I in the presence of the energies of the Thrones of I Am That I Am and YHWH, who have accompanied us. We begin to spin, imploding into the Throne of God-Source. Cobalt-Blue Light begins to explode around us as we bathe in the energies of the Throne of God-Source. Pause and breathe the Cobalt-Blue Light into your lungs.

Spinning upward, we will stop at the fifty-fifth dimension of reality to gather momentum and to connect with the energies of the Elohim. This is the Throne of Ellah, E-ll-a-h. The Elohim are the architects of this entire Universe. These Great Cosmic Beings brought this Universe into manifest form. They reside at this Throne of reality and beyond. The Light of the Throne and the presence of the Elohim welcome us. We all form a circle; you and St. Germain, Sanat Kumara and Uriel, the presence of the I Am, YHWH and God-Source. We are in Oneness as we stand around at the Golden-White Light of the Throne of Ellah.

We begin to spin and the spin becomes faster. The pull of gravity from the Throne of Ellah will move us to its center to implode into it and unite with it. Implosion leads to explosion and the process repeats three times.

The Universal Logos, Lord Melchizedek joins us. He is the great cosmic being whose consciousness over-lights this entire Universe. The Seven Mighty Elohim come forth to join our circle at this Throne. We merge into the essence of Lord Melchizedek. Brilliant Golden-White Light emanates everywhere as we bathe in the Light. Pause and breathe.

Spiraling upward inside the Pillar of Light we begin ascending. Gaining momentum, we reach the Throne of the Undifferentiated Source where all is Pure White Light. This is White Light before it went through the prism to become fractured or differentiated. This Throne is vast. It expands in every direction, like a canopy of Light.

We stand under the canopy in our Grid of Light formation, joined by our entourage together with the energies of Lord Melchizedek, the Seven Mighty Elohim and the energies of the Throne of Ellah. We begin to spin. The spin gains momentum to become faster. This time we are pulled upward into the center of the canopy to merge and unite with the essence of the Undifferentiated Source at the hundred and eighth Realm of Reality. Pause and feel the joy of this union. Breathe and feel the bliss of this experience.

We spiral upward to reach the Throne of Paramatman Light. It resides in its absolute pure essence at the one hundred twenty-second Realm. We spin into the Light of Paramatman and bring this Light with us.

We move from the Throne of Paramatman to go before the Throne of Absolute. The Throne of Absolute is the residence of Divine Mother, the Feminine Force with which this entire Manifest Creation was created.

As we stand in total reverence and awe at this Throne, a feminine form begins to take shape at the center of the circle. The Divine Mother, who is the epitome of the Feminine Creative Force of the universe, will show herself in a form to you. It can be in the form of a female being, a female deity, living or ascended, or she might show you a face or a body that is made of fire or Light. You may not be able to see the features, yet you know and sense that the Divine Mother is beckoning you to go to the center of the circle.

I will accompany you to the center. We stand shoulder to shoulder before the presence of the Divine Mother, the Feminine Principle. I ask her to bestow upon you greater Inner Perception and the ability to establish clear Inner Verbal Communication with her and with the Masters. I ask her to remove and release whatever contracts or choices you have made out of pain, struggle, and fear which have caused you to stop seeing the Inner Realms. I ask the Divine Mother to remove the veil and restore your Inner Sight. She will lovingly and gently remove the veil and restore your sight under the guidance of Yahoweh-EL.

The Angelic Forces of Yahoweh-EL guard the Feminine Creative Light. These beings are the energy of the Holy Spirit. The Angelic Forces of Yahoweh-EL are drops from the ocean of the Feminine Aspect of Metatron. We are in the presence of the Divine Mother, guarded by the energies of the Legions of Yahoweh-EL.

Ask the Divine Mother to support you in all your projects. Ask her to help you on your path. Ask her to give you guidance and support and help you to surrender to her will. I ask her to free you from all dross, pain and struggle and accelerate you in all that is to be accomplished through you in alignment with your Divine Mission.

Take the hem of her dress, kneel before her and ask her to grant your wishes. She is gentle, loving and compassionate. She loves you and cares for all the plans and the projects that you have agreed to accomplish. Seek her guidance in your own words. Now appeal to her and say,

"I ask you to use me as your conduit, vehicle, catalyst to bring forth change; change for a greater good, change for greater service to the Light, change for the Reign of Light to begin, change for those who have been in hardship, those who have struggled, and those who have experienced pain. Give them the grace to have your presence in their lives; help them to fully and completely heal and unite their personality aspects with your presence as their guiding force. I stand before you with great devotion. I ask you to intercede on my behalf and call the Original Blueprint for the perfection of Light in this reality. Accelerate me on the path of perfection, and bring that perfection to Earth. Help me receive help and guidance from the Higher Realms through you. In the mundane realm bring the right people, places, and things into my life and my hands. I most especially ask for financial means, power, prosperity, unlimited supply of resources and abundance to serve you and the Light to bring perfection to my life and the lives of others."

I, St. Germain, ask my beloved Divine Mother to provide you with unlimited comfort and luxury. I ask Mother to help you gain humility and greater ability to focus on your Divine Mission. I ask for the intercession of the Divine Mother in all aspects of your life. I ask her to over-light you to help you become a Beacon of Light to illuminate the world. I ask Mother to eliminate all the dross and bring flows and streams of money, abundance and prosperity; people, places and things that will help accomplish all tasks; raising the consciousness of humankind and the consciousness of the planet and allowing the higher vibrational frequency of Light to shine upon all.

I ask my beloved Divine Mother, to bring forth the Force, Power and Might of the Seven Lords of Light. I hold my Scepter of Power over my head and ask you to do the same. I invite the Seven Mighty

Elohim, Lord Melchizedek, Lord Sanat Kumara, the Thrones of Absolute, Paramatman, Undifferentiated Source, Ellah, YHWH and I Am That I Am to join us in our prayers. I invite the Beings of Light from the Melchizedek Brotherhoods, the Legions of Michael, Uriel, Yahoweh-EL, Metatron, EL-Shaddai, the Mighty Elohim and the Legions of the Great Silent Watcher. I ask that every Scepter of Power be held over the head as a symbol of action, a symbol for holding up the torch, lighting the path and freeing everyone from pain and dross. I ask for the opening of the pathways of Light to all souls and to the planet. I ask for the raising of the consciousness of the planet and the consciousness of humankind. For the benefit of Light, for the greater good of all souls, for the Ascension of Earth and for love to fully reign on Earth, I offer you all that I am and all that I have done in service, my beloved Divine Mother, and I ask that my reward be given to all who serve you. I thank you for all that you do for humankind.

Let us stay here and receive the shower of blessings from the Divine Mother, the Mighty Elohim, the Great Silent Watchers, the Legions of Michael and Yahoweh-EL, Metatron, EL-Shaddai, Melchizedek, Ancient of Days, all the Thrones and all the Light. Pause and bathe in the Light.

We hold every one of these great beings in our heart as we ask permission to leave the Throne of Absolute. We spiral down from the presence of the Divine Mother back to the Throne of Paramatman and further down to Undifferentiated Source. Blessing these Thrones and being blessed by them, we begin descending in the Pillar of Light to the Throne of Ellah and the Seven Mighty Elohim and continue spiraling down further to the Throne of God-Source, Throne of YHWH and the Throne of I Am That I Am. Blessing the Thrones and receiving Light and a shower of strength, we bow down before the presence of Sanat Kumara and ask him to over-light our body, our being, our nervous system and our Five Body System.

We spiral down to the consciousness of the body. I stand before you with my left hand on your Heart Chakra. The Sphere of Illumination is fully active, beaming Light to your Heart Chakra. The spin slows down to stop. You are able to see the Purple Ball of Light and the Flame inside.

I ask you to visualize the Flame inside of this Sphere at all times and focus on it many times during the course of each day. Keep it moving and energize it to spin to where it turns to Peach-Pink activating your body, cell structure and DNA to heal you and to transmute all that no longer serves you.

I ask you to visualize a spiral of Violet Flame. Imagine that you and I are together standing inside an enormous tongue of Violet Flame. It spirals from the base of your feet upward, moving counter-clockwise around you and up.

The Violet Flame must always be encountered from the Earth to the Heavens above and it must always be spun counter-clockwise. The spinning in counter-clockwise direction will help transmute all the dross from all the eons of lifetimes of struggle and the immediate daily dross from people, places and things. Always wrap yourself in the Violet Flame before you embark on the events of each day. Before you get out of bed, visualize yourself standing in front of St. Germain. His left hand is on your heart beaming you Light. The Violet Flame is moving counter-clockwise with Purple Light spinning all around you. Start your day and end your day in this way.

At night when you lay down say, *"I ask St. Germain to take me to his chosen retreat tonight."* I will take you to the Retreat of the Ascension Flame over Zurich, the Retreat of God-Unity at the Throne of the Divine Mother, the Retreat of Luxor with the Flame of Ascension, and to Shamballa where Sanat Kumara resides.

I hold you in my own heart with great reverence, with great love, with great joy for this union.

I am your very own St. Germain,
your own brother, your own father, your own best friend, and your beloved. So it is.

"I call upon Quan Yin, I ask for the energies of Purity and Innocence to permanently imbue my life. I call upon Goddess Hecate to fill me with power, passion, Life Force and positive action. I call upon Mother Mary to fill me with love, peace, harmony and happiness."

Goddess Hecate

CHAPTER IX

Manifestation

In this chapter, Goddess Hecate has blessed us with a candle grid to accelerate the manifestation of greater events in both the mundane and in the spiritual spectrum of our lives. Quan Yin and Mother Mary are invited to be our guardians along with Goddess Hecate. Through their combined energies, we have the chance to experience greater love, peace and harmony.

It would be best to make a written list of all your intentions and place it by the grid. Recite these intentions each time you light the candles. This will accelerate the manifestation process by the fact that your focused intent is upon those intensions at each lighting of the candles. Focus on your Heart Chakra when making the intentions and for each subsequent recitation, say your intensions out loud if possible, with love and fervor. Feel the energy of love surrounding you each time you repeat them.

May you experience joy and success in empowering yourself to manifest all your intentions from this moment on with the blessing of Goddess Hecate, Lady Quan Yin and Mother Mary.

Yin yang is a symbol which brings the polarities into equilibrium. The white and the black are signs of the duality of Light and Dark and the polarities of Male and Female.

My Children of Light I am Hecate.

I would like to give you a candle grid. With this candle grid you will manifest greater acceleration of all actions and events in your mundane and spiritual life through inviting Goddess Hecate, Lady Quan Yin and Mother Mary to become your guardians. Their guardianship can influence your life bringing greater Life Force, positive action, purity, love, joy, and greater spiritual growth to your life.

It is best to meditate in order to formulate your intentions and desires and then to write them all down. You can set up this grid for one or more intentions, be they spiritual or mundane. For example, for the healing of body, mind, and spirit, acceleration of spiritual growth, service to the Masters, or a new job, a new house, for the sale of an existing home, the outcome of an interview, test or exam, the resolution of a legal matter, manifestation of money, relationships, or partnerships.

In this grid you will use one red candle, one white candle and one pink candle. The red candle is for passion and power, the white, for purity and innocence and the pink for love. With a red felt tip pen, draw a triangle on a white sheet of paper or on a white poster board. The triangle can be an equilateral one. Each side of the triangle can be nine inches long. Inside the center of this triangle draw a circle approximately the size of a dollar coin (one inch diameter). Inside the circle draw the sign of yin yang. Yin yang is a symbol which brings the polarities into equilibrium. The white and the black are signs of the duality of Light and Dark and the polarities of Male and Female.

Place a mound of cinnamon over the entire small circle of yin-yang in the middle. Draw a large circle around the entire triangle. The three points of the triangle must touch the edge of the circle. Place the three candles of white, red, and pink at the three points of the triangle. Sprinkle cinnamon around the perimeter of the large outer circle. The cinnamon will absorb into your grid the object of your desire and seal your intention into the candle grid. When you place the cinnamon in the center over the sign of the yin-yang, you are overcoming polarity and duality. The negativity is transmuted by the cinnamon and the positive charge of the candle grid permeates into your life and your environment.

The cinnamon sprinkled around the large outer circle symbolizes the encircling of your desires and intentions. It magnifies the effect of the three candles at each point of the triangle. The triangle is the sign of the Triune Aspect. Your world has been brought forth through the trinity of the Mother-Father-Child. These three aspects balance your world and bring the Creative Force into manifest form. The white candle represents the purity of the Child Aspect. It is the symbol of the birthing of the New; a new plan, project, idea or event. The pink candle represents the love of the Mother Aspect. It manifests your intentions through the Creative Force of the Feminine. The red candle represents passion and action. It symbolizes the active Male Energy, the Father aspect. Through the active passion of the Male Force, all things come to manifest form. All three candles will help to birth your ideas or desires and bring them to manifestation.

Place your candle grid in a private location where it can remain unmoved and undisturbed for the duration of the exercise. Once you have set up your grid and formulated your intentions, begin the process of imbuing your grid with your intentions. This means that you place your specific intentions into the candle grid. While the candle grid is lit, your intentions will permeate through the grid into your environment. They will impact the Five Elements of Earth, Water, Fire, Air, and Ether to accelerate the manifestation of your intentions. The fire from the candle flames and the cinnamon helps to transmute the obstacles. The colors of the candles carry symbolic meanings: white for innocence, pink for love, and red for passion and action.

It is important to have clarity about what you want. State those intentions clearly and write them down. Place it by your candle grid. Every time you light your grid, read those intentions in order exactly as you did the first time.

Lighting the Candle Grid for the First Time

Once you have formed your intentions and have placed your candle grid in its permanent position, do the following:

Pick up the white candle and hold it up. Call upon Quan Yin saying, *"I invoke Quan Yin to imbue this white candle with the energies of purity and innocence. I ask for the energies of purity and innocence to permanently imbue my life."* Place the white candle back at its point. Quan Yin becomes the guardian of the white candle and the qualities that you have requested.

Pick up the red candle and say, *"I call upon Goddess Hecate to imbue this candle with power, passion, Life Force and positive action in my life."* Place the red candle back at its point. Hecate becomes the guardian of the red candle and the qualities that you have requested.

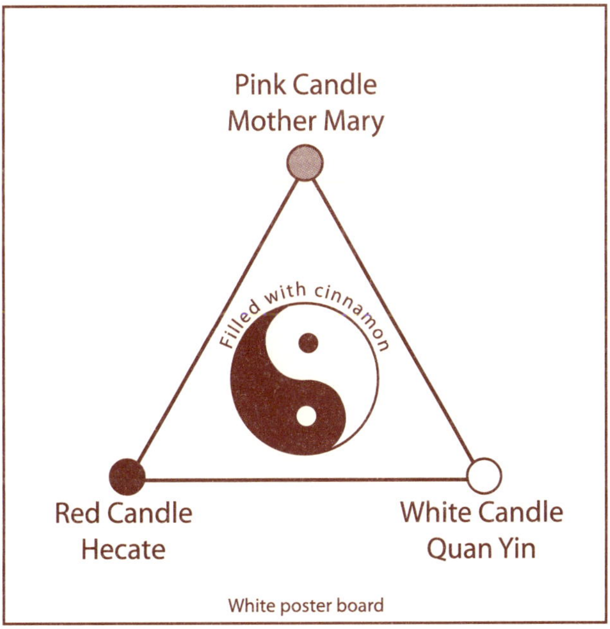

Pick up the pink candle and call upon Mother Mary and say, *"I call upon Mother Mary to imbue this pink candle with energies of love, peace, harmony and happiness to permanently permeate my life and my being."* Mother Mary becomes the guardian of the pink candle and the qualities you have requested.

Begin the process of imbuing your grid with your intentions. Read your intentions out loud and offer them to the grid. Say, *"I imbue this candle grid with the following intentions…"*

This means that you place your specific intentions into the candle grid. When lit, your intentions permeate in the air through the energies of the grid. The fire of the candles and the cinnamon helps to transmute the obstacles. The symbolic meaning of the colors of the candles helps bring those aspects; purity and innocence, passion and action and love to the grid and to you. The circle absorbs and magnifies the intentions. Repeated lighting of the candle grid adds momentum to your intention, magnifying its impact and accelerating its manifestation.

Start lighting the candles in a clockwise direction. When you go in a clockwise direction you bring energy into the grid. If you were making a grid to release something, then you would light the candles in counter-clockwise fashion; for example, to release a disease or to release karma. This grid, however, is not for those types of intentions. It is effective as a manifestation grid for bringing things or situations to you. Every time you re-light your candle grid, say the above invocations and state your intentions.

Do this grid for a set number of days; for example, twenty-two days, or a full month, or even three months for your long term intentions. If one set of candles burns out, start new ones. If you manifest your desires and the first set of candles are still burning, it is best to burn them out completely. You can use the same poster board and the cinnamon to continue with other intentions as the energy of the grid builds up. For this reason it is best to use larger pillar candles, for example 3"x 9" pillar or 1.5"x 6" pillar candles. Sometimes the candle wax spills over the poster board. Pick up the pieces, clean the board and continue using it. Every time you start a new set of candles, repeat the setting up process (say the invocations printed above under Lighting the Candle Grid for the First Time). It is more powerful to say the invocation to each deity (Hecate, Quan Yin and Mother Mary) every time you light the candle grid and then state or read your intentions. If you can sit for meditation for ten or fifteen minutes while the grid is lit, the process will be accelerated even further. You may extinguish the candles after this period or leave them burning if you can make sure that they do not pose a fire hazard.

When you have completed your candle grid, it is best if you can throw the cinnamon into running water, such as the ocean or a stream. You can also sprinkle it in your flower or vegetable garden.

My beloved children, call upon me to come to your aid at all times. Remember that I stand by your side to help you and guide you.

I am your mother, Hecate.

Summary of Candle Grid for Manifestation

- Draw the diagram shown here on a white poster board with a red felt-tip pen.
- Pour a mound of cinnamon to cover the entire sign of the yin-yang.
- Sprinkle cinnamon around the perimeter of the large circle.

- Place the three candles; one red, one white, and one pink, at the three points of the triangle.
- Once you have formed your intentions and have placed your candle grid in its permanent position, do the following:
- Pick up the white candle and hold it up. Call upon Quan Yin saying, *"I invoke Quan Yin to imbue this white candle with the energies of purity and innocence. I ask for the energies of purity and innocence to permanently imbue my life."* Place the white candle back at its point. Quan Yin becomes the guardian of the white candle and the qualities that you have requested.
- Now pick up the red candle and say, *"I call upon Goddess Hecate to imbue this candle with power, passion, Life Force and positive action in my life."* Place the red candle back at its point. Hecate becomes the guardian of the red candle and the qualities that you have requested.
- Now pick up the pink candle and call upon Mother Mary and say, *"I call upon Mother Mary to imbue this pink candle with energies of love, peace, harmony and happiness to permanently permeate my life and my being."* Mother Mary becomes the guardian of the pink candle and the qualities you have requested.
- Begin the process of imbuing your grid with your intentions. Read your intentions out loud and offer them to the grid. Say, *"I imbue this candle grid with the following intentions..."*
- Print out the invocations and add your intentions in written form. Place this by the side of your candle

grid. Every time you light your grid say the invocations and your intentions out loud.

After the first time, it is sufficient to simply read the invocations and intentions to yourself. You do not have to pick up each candle after the first time.

Do this grid for nine days, or twenty-two days, or even three months if you have long term intentions. If one set of candles burns out, start new ones. If the duration of your grid is completed and the first set of candles is still burning, allow those candles to burn out completely.

You can use the same poster board and cinnamon to continue as the energy of the grid is building up. For this reason it is best to use larger pillar candles, for example 3"x 9" pillar or 1.5"x 6" pillar candles.

If the candle wax spills over the poster board, pick up the pieces, clean the board and continue using it. Every time you start a new set of candles repeat the setting up process over.

When you have completed your candle grid, it is best if you can throw the cinnamon into running water, such as the ocean or a stream. You can also sprinkle it in your flower or vegetable garden.

"I call upon the essence of the Divine Mother,
the Feminine Principle of Existence to overlay
a nervous system and a Five Body System, which she has
prepared for me, upon my body and nervous system.
I ask the Divine Mother, the Feminine Principle,
to recalibrate my nervous system and my Five Body System
to unfold my acceleration with ease, peace and harmony,
to accomplish the release of karma and all karmic
entanglements and to fully prepare me to serve the Light."

Goddess Hecate

CHAPTER X

Life in Service to Christ Maitreya

In this exercise, Goddess Hecate brings us before the Throne of Divine Mother and intercedes on our behalf to receive a new template for a strong and sustaining nervous system to be overlaid upon ours and to illuminate our Five Body System. A powerful Magnification Candle Grid follows where we ask for the release of all karma and karmic entanglements remaining in this lifetime to be transmuted by Goddess Hecate, Sanat Kumara and Metatron. Hecate beckons us to offer our life in service to Christ Maitreya. By his presence on Earth, Christ Maitreya has offered his life in service to earth and all souls. By interweaving our Divine Mission with his, we can not only fulfill our Divine Mission but also stand in his service to fulfill his Divine Mission.

As we become more spiritually evolved, our needs change. Our energy bodies, including our physical body, become more sensitive to all stimuli. Being in the world and functioning from the higher vibrational force field can take its toll on us. It is not easy to be connected to the Higher Realms and move high Quotients of Light through our body to anchor on earth and yet remain fully focused on the mundane. This exercise is a gift from Divine Mother to help us at a point when important planetary energies were brought forth to be anchored on earth, while we were simultaneously in the throes of coping with deadlines for completion of the Path to Enlightenment books and overhauling our website. While both of these projects were in essence a service to the Light and the Masters, one required a withdrawal from the world to be still and receive the heightened energies; while the other required our full focus on embracing the mundane and being present in every moment.

Divine Mother gave us this gift to help us cope and manage both projects to perfection while keeping our sanity!

I wish you great joy in receiving the overlaying of Divine Mother's Light over your nervous system and the illumination of her Light upon your Five Body System while you offer your life in service to Christ Maitreya.

My Child of Light, I am Hecate.

I hold you in my Divine embrace. The time has come for great acceleration. The most effective way to accelerate yourself is to accomplish your Divine Mission. This is the highest path that you can take in service to the Light. Your Divine Mission should be your highest objective. This objective can best be served when you offer yourself in service to Christ Maitreya, the World Teacher. The Masters of Wisdom and Christ Maitreya are calling upon their Disciples to gather.

My children, I love you with all my heart. I am interceding on your behalf before the presence of Christ Maitreya. Before he comes out to the multitudes and masses, he is going to gather the sheep of his flock around him. I want you to volunteer to be called. Then he will intercede on your behalf. For this to happen, you must free yourself of all dross, distractions and delays. He will then absorb and transmute what remains of your karma and karmic entanglements with people, places and things. It also means a great acceleration of your life and the raising of your Quotient of Light. To achieve this feat, Christ Maitreya will help you shrink down your karma and Karmic entanglements for this lifetime.

This plan may take a year to fully unfold. During this time you will live each month of this year as the equivalent of a decade or even more. In the first part of the year he will help you to be free from personal karma. This is so that in the second part of the year, you can build your Light to higher quotients to enable you to withstand his Light and to serve him. Think of a six month phase that would be six decades worth of your life. There would be times in the course of the six months, from the point that you take this vow, to offer your life in his service, when you may feel burdened by the rate of this acceleration. This is why I give you the following Magnification Grid of Light. By making this grid you call upon your mother Hecate, Sanat Kumara and Metatron to intercede on your behalf and release the burden of this acceleration from your life. To further the impact, you can have the grid continue to be active for the first six months after you take this vow.

This is what you have worked to gain over many lifetimes; to rush yourself to this point. The point when he arrives to gather the sheep of his flock. You are one of them. He has already ordained it.

Otherwise I would not be offering you this Grid of Light to take the vow of offering your life in his service. When he comes, no struggle for survival in the mundane realms would ever be an issue again. If you have not worked them out, he will do it for you. If there is any darkness around or within you, that darkness will eat you up and he will not allow it. That is why I have offered you my help. I have told you to put me in the point at the South in your candle grid. The South represents the Darkness, Earth and Feminine. I have called upon Metatron and Sanat Kumara to be my helpers. What is important is not the triangle but the candle in the center which holds the energies of Christ Maitreya, the Seven Lords of Light and Maha Lord of Light. The Lords of Light have come back to Earth after thousands of years. They have come back to be his helpers. They have come to bring the Light which he needs in order to present himself to humankind. For that to happen, he first needs to gather those who will be his anchors, his helpers, the Beacons of Light. On that Light he must ride in order to succeed.

By offering yourself in his service, you are asking for everything that you are to be dedicated and devoted to his Light. Then you shall become much vaster than what you are now. This is because in his presence the planet and all souls can hold greater Light and greater wisdom. This is another level of acceleration added to the candle grid. This way you can tune into the Mind of God, the Quantum Pool of Wisdom at the Throne of Creation and the body of the Feminine Principle. This body of Creation is Manifest and made of the warp and weft of the body of the Feminine Principle. Say,

"I call upon the essence of the Divine Mother, the Feminine Principle of Existence to overlay a nervous system and a Five Body System, which she has prepared for me, upon my body and nervous system. I ask the Divine Mother, the

Feminine Principle, to recalibrate my nervous system and my Five Body System to unfold my acceleration with ease, peace and harmony, to accomplish the release of karma and all karmic entanglements and to fully prepare me to serve the Light."

This invocation is very important. Every morning say this prayer and repeat it every night. The nervous system and Five Body System will be an extension of the body and nervous system of the Divine Mother. It will allow you to accelerate yourself to handle the karma of six decades in six months.

Therefore you are connecting to an essence of yourself which is much greater than your present nervous system and your Five Body System. With these, you accelerate your own vibration beyond the norm on Earth. The analogy would be to say that, with this new system of energy bodies and nervous system, you will be able to run two hundred volts of electricity through a cable which could only handle five volts before. To adjust, you may call upon me or any essence of the Divine Mother at any time.

I love you with all of my heart. Understand that the moment you perform the first ceremony for setting up this grid and lighting the candle, you will feel relieved as though someone has taken a huge burden off of your shoulders. You have come into this lifetime with deep and vast intentions as part of your Soul Mission and have been in service to this planet for eons of time. When you take no respite in between lifetimes, your soul becomes weary and your heart heavy. It is normal to take two to three hundred years of respite in between each lifetime. This allows the soul a chance to rest. Then the pain, fears, struggles and the dross of each lifetime do not get carried over to the next. For several lifetimes you have had your next body prepared for your entry before you exited the last one. This can inflict a shock to the imprint of your energy bodies and affect your present nervous system.

As a result, you may feel alienated from people; feeling that no one understands what you go through. With the overlaying of the new nervous system and Five Body System offered to you by Divine Mother, you will be able to integrate yourself to a greater extent, both into the mundane and the sublime.

Magnification Candle Grid

Now I offer you the Magnification Candle Grid. Set this candle grid on a black poster board. The black color will help to absorb the dross to itself. Use a gold pen for this grid as gold has alchemical potencies which brings strength from the Heavenly Realms, helps to anchor those energies in the Earthly realms and transmutes all obstacles on its way. Draw a large circle on the black poster board with the gold pen. Then draw an equilateral triangle inside the circle. From the edge of the candle to each side of the triangle there needs to be two inches distance. Position this drawing so that one point of the triangle sits in the direction of South. On that point write Hecate with gold pen and place a piece of hematite crystal over it. Hematite also helps to pull the dross out and absorb it to itself. The other two points will sit in the direction of Northwest and Northeast. Write down Metatron in the Northwest and place a small clear quartz crystal on top. In the Northeast write down Sanat Kumara and place another piece of clear quartz crystal on top of Sanat Kumara's name in the Northeast point.

Draw a small circle at the center inside of the triangle and in that central circle write down "Christ Maitreya." Pour a mound of cinnamon on top of that circle over Christ Maitreya's name. Cinnamon absorbs the objects of your desires to you. In this case the objective is to pull the energies of Christ Maitreya into your life. Flatten the cinnamon and place the candle on top. The candle can be inside a round jar. It is important that the candle has three wicks. The three flames represent Hecate, Metatron and Sanat Kumara and they are connected to each other by the body of the candle. These three are the guardians of this candle. The candle should be inside a round jar. The candle and the container must be round. Oval is acceptable, round is better. A square candle is not good in this case, because the square angles can hold on to the stagnant energies and disperse them to the grid.

Follow the instructions that I have given you. The invocations below are of great importance. Write them down and carry them around with you during the course of the day to repeat when you can. Place a printed copy by your candle grid. Read it out loud with full intent, zest and fervor at each lighting of the candles

Materials Needed

- Large round red candle with three flames (approximately 6" diameter) (Oval is acceptable, square is not acceptable).
- Black poster board, approximately 18"x 18" or larger.
- Gold pen.
- 1 Hematite crystal
- 2 clear Quartz crystals
- Cinnamon

How to Draw Your Grid

- Draw a gold circle around the circumference of the candle in the center of the poster board.

- Draw an equilateral triangle in gold around the large candle. Allowing a minimum clearance of 2" from the edge of the candle to the sides of the triangle.
- Write *Hecate* in gold on the South point and place a piece of Hematite crystal on that point.
- Write *Metatron* in gold on the Northwest point and place a piece of clear Quartz crystal on that point.
- Write *Sanat Kumara* in gold on the Northeast point and place a piece of clear Quartz crystal on that point.
- Write *Christ Maitreya* in gold in the center of the candle circle and place mound of cinnamon on top.
- Flatten the mound of cinnamon and place the candle (in a glass container) on top.
- Position the grid so that Goddess Hecate and the Hematite piece are sitting in the direction of South. This is important. Once in place, do not move the Candle Grid as a vortex of Light and Power is created in that place and the energies gain momentum with each lighting of the candles.

When the grid is complete and you have placed it in position, begin lighting the 3 flames.

Lighting the Candles

- Say, *"I light this flame in the name of Christ Maitreya, calling Hecate."* Light the first flame, in the position of South.
- Then say, *"I light this flame in the name of Christ Maitreya, calling Metatron."* Light the second flame, in the position of Northwest.

- Then say, *"I light this flame in the name of Christ Maitreya, calling Sanat Kumara."* Light the third flame, in the position of Northeast.
- Then say,

"I imbue this candle grid with the energies of the Seven Lords of Light and the Maha Lord of Light. I ask that the Seven Lords of Light and Maha Lord of Light continue to support the work of Christ Maitreya. I call the Seven Lords of Light and Maha Lord of Light into my life as Guardians of Light and I offer myself in service to them. I light this candle grid with the intent that all that remains of my life is now offered in service to Christ Maitreya, the Seven Lords of Light and the Maha Lord of Light. I ask that all karma and karmic entanglements remaining from this lifetime be absorbed and transmuted through Hecate, Metatron, Sanat Kumara, Christ Maitreya, the Seven Lords of Light, and the Maha Lord of Light, and I specifically ask Christ Maitreya to take what remains of this life and make it his. I offer myself in service to the Light."

My Children, remember that I stand by your side at all times. You may call upon The Divine Mother in all your endeavors, in all circumstances and at all times. I ask you to seriously continue the lighting of this grid and the repetition of the invocational prayers for a six month period of time. Make a commitment to yourself to carry this task to its completion.

With all the love in my heart, I stand by your side and guide you.

I am your mother Hecate. So it is. Blessed be.

"Mother help me find ideas, designs and thought forms
which will come into manifestation and serve me well,
make my life easier and take me further on my spiritual path."

Metatron

CHAPTER XI

Journey to the Thrones

In thanksgiving for what we have accomplished, Metatron takes us to each of the Thrones of Light to ask for prosperity and abundance. When we arrive at the Throne of Absolute, in the Presence of Divine Mother, Metatron reminds us of the importance of our Free Will in choosing to serve the Divine Mother. The importance of choosing, *"not my will but Thy will be done,"* and accepting the Pure and Innocent Feminine Child Seed into our hearts.

Our Free Will has lead us to forget our Divine Mission and feel separate from our Divine Origin. By offering our Free Will to be replaced by the Divine Will we can bring ourselves and our world back to the purity of the Original Intent. *"Not my will but Thy Will be done"* is the epitome of the ultimate state of God-Unity.

Beloveds of my own heart, I am Metatron.

Take a deep breath with me. Focus your energy at the center of your Cosmic Heart Chakra. Visualize yourself standing before Metatron. Visualize Legions of Michael standing around us with their Swords of Mercy. The Swords are Pillars of Aquamarine-Blue Light. They stand shoulder to shoulder with their arms outstretched holding their Swords of Mercy over our heads. Visualize, from the touching of the points of the Swords of Mercy, a shower of Aquamarine-Blue Light begins to pour down upon us. This Blue Light is the Light of Empowerment, the Light of Mercy, and the Light of Protection. Power, Mercy and Protection are pouring down upon us. Visualize that a Bubble of Light is forming around us.

I will take you on a journey to the Throne of Creation to go before the Presence of the Divine Mother. From the Divine Mother, who is the Feminine Principle of Existence, and the Creative Force of this entire Creation, I will ask prosperity and abundance for you. We will take a journey through the Thrones of God, manifest and non-manifest and visit deities and hierarchies of Great and Cosmic Beings of Light. At these Thrones we ask for a blessing and pause a moment to express our intentions at each one. We will invite every member of every throne to accompany us to the Throne of the Divine Mother.

The Bubble of Blue Light is now formed. I call forth the Great Silent Watcher, who is the God-Mother for this entire creation. She held the design and idea for this Earth and the Solar System in her heart for millions of years until it became a reality. I will ask her that every one of your intentions be realized. You can repeat this exercise from this moment on everyday as many times as you desire. You can write your list of desires and place it in the grid formation.

Call upon the Great Silent Watcher, ask her to hold those intentions in her heart and bless you with favorable results. I invoke Goddess Lakshmi, the Goddess of Abundance and Prosperity in spiritual as well as in material matters. To achieve the objects of your desires, you must work with Goddess Lakshmi. She sits on the treasure chest of all resources of Earth. She also sits on the treasure chest of the heavenly realms and brings you spiritual abundance.

Now I ask Goddess Lakshmi to join me at the very center of this circle. Visualize that you and Lakshmi are facing each other and make a triangle with Metatron. Around the outer circle the Legions of Michael stand shoulder to shoulder emanating Aquamarine-Blue Light of Power, Mercy and Protection. Together, we are creating Prosperity, Abundance, Success, and Power. To do this we call upon our beloved Great Silent Watcher, the true Mother for this Earth and Solar System. You can always call upon her as the true Creative Force.

The Great Silent Watcher creates another layer in the form of a large Bubble of Aquamarine-Blue interspersed with Emerald-Green, to manifest prosperity. Emerald-Green is the color of truth and hope. It is also the color for manifestation of physical abundance on Earth. Green is a color most abundant in nature. It emanates the energy of healing. Everything in this third dimensional realm of reality can be healed and manifested through the Emerald-Green Ray. Breathe into your lungs this Emerald-Green Ray, interspersed with the Aquamarine-Blue Light which the Great Silent Watcher, is showering upon you now.

Focus your attention on Goddess Lakshmi and feel her Presence. She comes in her majesty clad in red robes with a golden tiara over her head. From her wrist all the way up her arm she is wearing gold bangles. Around her neck she wears gold. Red and Gold are the colors that Goddess Lakshmi brings. Gold represents the alchemy of the Heavenly Realm and Red is the Life Force of Earth; the Life Force that beats and pulses through your veins. Now visualize that the Aquamarine-Blue and Emerald-Green Bubble is spinning around you. We move spiraling outside of the consciousness of this body. I invoke the Pillar of Pure White Light to form around you and the Bubble of Aquamarine-Blue and Emerald-Green Light. The Pillar of Pure White Light is fully formed and we spiral upward inside it. Each of you has a cord of Light, which extends from the top of your head and connects you to the Higher Realms. Visualize that your cord is now emanating White Light as we begin spiraling upwards.

We reach the Throne of the I Am That I Am, God-in form, and we bless the Throne. It is emanating Brilliant Light. Your own individualized essence is now merging into the presence of the I Am at the Throne. Pause, breathe and bathe in this Light.

We invite the Presence of the I Am to accompany us as we spiral upward to the next Throne, the Throne of YHWH. This Throne is emanating Gold Liquid Light. Enter the Throne and merge into the Golden Light and invite the presence of YHWH to unite with you. Pause and bathe in the Light. Breathe deeply.

We ask the presence of YHWH to accompany us. We spiral upward in the company of YHWH and the I Am to the Throne of God-Source.

Cobalt-Blue Light is emanating from this Throne. Immerse yourself in the Cobalt-Blue Light of the God-Source. We merge and unite in Oneness with the God-Source. Pause and breathe as you bathe in God-Source Energies.

We invite the Being of this Throne to accompany us. In the presence of the I Am That I Am, YHWH and God-Source we spiral upwards to the Throne of Ellah. This is the residence of the Elohim, the architects of this Universe. This is where Pure White Light begins to fully emanate as Form fades into Semi-Form, the half-way point on the journey from Form to Non-Form. In the presence of the I Am That I Am, YHWH and God-Source, we merge into the Throne of Ellah. We pause to receive the full essence. Breathe and bathe in the Light.

Ellah will accompany us, spiraling upwards, as we move to the Throne of Undifferentiated Source. This is God in Non-Form. This is God as essence, energy and indescribable Light. The Throne of Undifferentiated Source is Pure Love. We spiral into this Throne and ask the presence of Undifferentiated Source to bless and fill every iota, molecule, cell, and particle of our being. Pause and bathe to absorb the energies.

In the company of the I Am, YHWH, God-Source, Ellah and the Undifferentiated Source we move up to the Throne of Paramatman. Atman is the Realized Self. Paramatman is that which is beyond the Realized Self, the Supreme Self, the Self of all Selves. Here the colors change. There is a touch of Aquamarine-Blue. In the company of the I Am, YHWH, God-Source, Ellah and Undifferentiated Source, we bathe in the Light of Paramatman. Pause and absorb the energies. Bathe and breathe in the Light.

We ask Paramatman to join us as we move to the Throne of the Seven Lords of Light and the Maha Lord of Light. The emanations of this Throne are Aquamarine-Blue mixed with Platinum Light. Platinum is the energy of the Maha Lord of Light, for he carries the essence of the Divine Mother in its purest form. He brings the essence of the Platinum Light of the Creative Force of the Feminine to Earth, encapsulated in the Masculine. The Aquamarine-Blue is the essence that is over-lighting that Throne because there are Seven Lords.

The First Lord emanates Blue-Green; the Second Lord, Yellow-Peach; the Third Lord, Red; the Fourth Lord, Aquamarine-Blue; the Fifth Lord, Emerald-Green; the Sixth Lord, Bright Orange and the Seventh Lord, Purple-Magenta. The united forces of the Seven Lords are over-lighted by the Aquamarine-Blue. Why? Because the Aquamarine-Blue is the color for the Feminine Principle when it takes form to become a Masculine Essence in order to come to Earth and unfold as the Seventh Golden Age. Through the Guardianship of the Seven Lords of Light and the Maha Lord of Light, this event will become a reality. The over-lighting color to symbolize it is Aquamarine-Blue interspersed with Platinum Light. Immerse yourself at the Throne of the Seven Lords of Light and the Maha Lord of Light with the Platinum energies interspersed with Aquamarine-Blue and bless the presence of everyone who has accompanied you here. Breathe and bathe in the Light.

We join together to go to the Throne of Absolute and stand before the Divine Mother. Divine Mother resides upon three layers of reality close to the 144th Realm. She has three specific Thrones. The first one is the Throne of Absolute. The next one is the Pool of Creation and the third one is the Pure Essence of the Feminine Principle. We stand before the Divine Mother at the Throne of Absolute and ask her to grant us permission and bless us to be taken to the Throne of Creation. Pause and bathe in the energies of Absolute.

We are brought to the Throne of Creation in the company of Divine Mother. Now we ask permission to enter the Pool of Creation. All Creation, Ideas, Designs, Concepts, are held inside of this Pool in seed form.

This is a planet of free will. You have your own free will. For as long as you choose to keep your free will, I need to ask you permission to set out intentions on your behalf; even though doing it my way would probably be more beneficial for you than doing it your way, I still have to ask you. I know what is good for you and I can do it for you. However, unless you say, *"Not my will, but Thy will be done,"* none of us, not even the Divine Mother can do anything for you. You have to ask for our help before we can intercede on your behalf. Do not think that because we know what is best for you we can automatically give it to you. This is why you have been told, *"Ask and you shall receive."*

Do not say, *"Well, you know what I want, do it for me,"* but instead, specifically state what you want and then say, *"This is what I want, do this or better."* When you choose to say, *"Not my will, but Thy will be done,"* then you have given us a free hand. There may be something better that we can do for you but unless you say "this or better," we cannot give it to you. Then you have to accept and surrender. When I will something for you, you cannot throw a tantrum at me and say, *"Ha, I did not want it this way. I wanted it the way I thought I wanted it."* That will not do. If you give up your will, then know that the will of the Divine can take care of you better than your limited free will can. Therefore, if you decide to give up your free will, it will do you great good, when you surrender to that Divine Will and accept what the Divine Will unfolds before you and allow yourself to see the merit. It is possible at first you will not see the merit. Yet, as you grow in Light, you learn what the Divine wants for you and recognize the merits. You may only be able to see a small part of the picture but the Divine has the panoramic landscape. When you are privy to seeing the panoramic landscape, then you will not throw any tantrums, then you will not be upset with me, or with the Divine Mother.

To have a peaceful life and to grow spiritually with utmost grace and gentleness, take the hem of the Divine Mother's robes and ask for her Divine Will. There is no deity and no greater Light Being that can be more compassionate and more forgiving than the Divine Mother. In this auspicious moment I take you before her. The rest is up to you. How you make her love you even more, how you get her attention, every minute of every day, how you dedicate and devote your life to her, how you get her to feel the love that you send to her and multiply that love and return it to you, is up to you. My job is to bring you here. You are here before her Throne. Sit and take the hem of her robes and say,

"Mother, give me permission right now. Take me to the Pool of Creation and help me find ideas, concepts, designs and thought-forms which will come into manifestation and serve me well; the ideas, designs, concepts, thought-forms, and actions that will make my life easier; the ideas, designs, concepts, and actions that will take me further on my spiritual path. Mother, I will not take no for an answer. I will stay here and hold the hem of your dress until you give me permission. Mother, I offer you my life. Mother, I offer you myself in service. Mother, it is all about you. You created it all. From you I have come and to you I shall return. Oh Mother, take me into your heart. Take me into your bosom. Forgive me for what I have done and remind me that I am Divine. Remind me that I am a particle of your Being. Remind me that I am great. Remind me that I am Light. Remind me that I walk with you. Remind me that I am not alone. Remind me that I am not abandoned. Remind me that you walk by my side. Mother, make my life easy. Show me the way. Plant the seed of the greatest alternate reality in my heart. Walk before me on my path. Over-light my body. Over-light my life. Over-light my loved ones. Over-light my spiritual path. Over-light my path in the mundane. Let me be your Light, Mother, hear me on this auspicious day. Help me do your work from this moment on, for I will do myself justice and I will do you justice to only hold the hem of your dress and only listen to your guidance for you are the Mother of all Mothers. I can go to no-one who will love me more than you will. I know it now."

You will see her as she wishes to appear to you. You may see her bedecked in red, in gold, in white, or in black. All colors belong to her. All Life Force belongs to her. All things belong to her. She created it all. Lucky are those who come to know that it is all about her. It is about you and it is about her. This whole Creation is all about her. This whole Creation has come about from her beingness. Every breath that she has taken takes form and is continuing to take form. As it takes form, you live that form; you become that form; you energize that form; you give life to that form, for you are a Divine Spark from her own heart.

Permission has been granted and the entourage of all the Thrones, who have also been kneeling before her, rise up. Accompanied by the Divine Mother, we all go to the Throne of Creation.

I especially call the Presence of Christ Maitreya, the World Teacher, who is the greatest Light blessing Earth. I also invite St. Germain, the Cohan of the Seventh Ray, the Master whose energy is now over-lighting Earth. It is through his body, his Light, his breath that you move from the density and the dross of the Age of Pisces, which did not become a Golden Age, to the Seventh Golden Age, the Age of Aquarius. Our beloved St. Germain, the Alchemist, now joins us. I invite the Seven Mighty Elohim to join us. I invite the Melchizedek Brotherhoods in the company of Lady Malak and Lord Melchizedek. I invite our Galactic Logos, Lord Melchior and Lady Melchai. I invite my dearly beloved brother whose Light is the consciousness of this planet, Sanat Kumara, and the entourage of the Seven Kumaras.

The Seven Kumaras came to rescue Earth many eons ago. See him walking, clad in his red robes. He is as brightly illumined as is my beloved Lakshmi. He too is wearing his beautiful Crown of Gold and his Red Robes, in your honor. For today is a day to glorify you. You have come to stand at the Throne of the Divine Mother and ask for the highest and the best reality to unfold for Earth and the multitudes and masses. You represent the multitudes and masses. You make a difference. That is the beauty of it. You can anchor the energy of prosperity and abundance for all who serve the Light on behalf of the Divine Mother. You can call upon Sanat Kumara whose consciousness is over-lighting the planet and say,

"From this moment on, I stand as your Beacon of Light, fully illumined by the energies of the Divine Mother."

To Christ Maitreya, the World Teacher, say,

"I stand as the Beacon of Light to spread your truth and hold space for your return to Earth, for your wisdom and your truth to spread on Earth, for your Physical Life Force and the Physical Life Force of the Masters of Wisdom to return to Earth."

I invite the Seven Mighty Elohim, who are the architects of this entire Creation, to come forth. I invite the Brotherhoods and the Sisterhoods of Light who reside in the White Lodge. I invite Master Thoth and Master Elyon and all the entourage and Beings from the planet Mercury. I invite him as Hermes. I invite him as Tahuti, the Egyptian and Thoth the Atlantean. I invite the energies of the height of the glory of Atlantis and Lemuria.

I invite Lord Buddha and Lady Quan Yin. Beloved Quan Yin has gently, quietly and lovingly carried the Violet Flame for 14,000 years. She finally passed the torch to our beloved St. Germain in this century. I invite Lord Buddha who has been the carrier and the Guardian of the energies of non-violence. I invite the essence and the presence of the living Masters, the living Avatars and I ask for their blessing. I ask you to devote and dedicate all the merits gained from this ceremony in service to the living Avatars. It is because of them that Light has returned to reign on Earth. They held that Light on Earth and prevented trauma and trouble to manifest in a form beyond manageable. I ask for a blessing for all of the living Avatars and the Ascended Masters. The living Avatars and Masters are owed more than the Ascended Masters because they sacrificed their physical bodies, their Life Force, their energy, their time and their Soul Lineage. They took on physical dense bodies to serve you. As their disciples, you too, have made a great sacrifice, and for that I honor you.

Together, we stand at the platform looking at the Pool of Creation. It looks like the deep, dark of the ocean on a Full Moon night. Every idea, thought form and concept that has ever existed before it becomes manifest, is in this Pool. We ask the Divine Mother for the Seed Thought-Form for the best alternate reality for you and your loved ones. For everyone that you touch, we ask for the best alternate reality to unfold. Imagine that! Not just your loved ones, not just your friends and your associates and your acquaintances, but everyone that you touch in any way.

That means that even when you engage in mundane things, when you go to the movie theater, you are Beacons of Light. When you go to a grocery store, you are Beacons of Light. The food on shelves would be raised in vibration. The food will then reach others and raise their vibration and help them live the utmost potential, the best alternate reality that they could ever desire or dream of living. Imagine the domino effect of this one intention. This is the intention I will set out for you. I ask you to sit still for a moment and visualize that with the Divine Mother's blessing, you call to yourself the Seeds of all those thoughts, designs, ideas and concepts which will become actions; actions which will unfold in your lives to serve the Light and you to the utmost, above and beyond limitation, above and beyond expectation. Say,

"Not my Will but Thy Will, for me, be done, Mother. Make me more glorious than I can even imagine. Give me more resources than I could even desire. Make me needless, not by making me suffer but make me needless by giving me so much that I will be the fruit bearing tree whose branches are pulled down because I am so filled with flowers and fruits."

Not the barren tree whose branches are shooting up to the stars thinking that she is really special. There is nothing special about a barren fruit tree except its arrogance. It is the humble fruit bearing tree that is full of Light and full of love and bubbling with the joy of all the fruits, all the babies that it carries. The branches are heavy and filled with Light, love and Life Force, with joy bubbling all around. That is the humble tree I want you to be. Ask that in her compassion, Divine Mother gives you everything and makes you humble. The more that you have, the more humble you will become, not because of hardship but because of love. Just like the children of the New Age. You look at them and you can feel the love emanating out of them. They have so much love that they bring the families together. That is what I want to see you do. I want to see that happen for you.

I want you to be like the Indigo children, the Crystal children, the Star children. Many names have been given to these very special souls. I want you to ask the Divine Mother to make you like them by making you needless. Needless because you have so much, you have no need of greed. You have no need of jealousy. You have no need to be envious. This is what I wish for you. This is what I am here to ask of her, on your behalf. I want to see that you have no need because you have no pain. All your pain is to be cleared in the Pool of Creation by her grace and compassion. Take a deep breath.

Start seeing yourself immersed inside the Pool of Creation. Liquid Light is all around you. It might feel like water or Light. It matters not how you feel it. What matters is to see yourself in the Pool of Creation knowing that the ionic particles of Creation are being magnetized to your body and being.

Visualize that you are pulling to yourself the charge of those designs, ideas, and concepts which will become actions of greatest service to you and through you to the world; greatest service to the Light, greatest service to Divine Mother, greatest service to Christ Maitreya, greatest service to Sanat Kumara, greatest service to St. Germain. Pull those thoughts, ideas, and concepts to yourself. Say,

"Not my Will, but Thy Will be done. I am surrendered to your Will. Will for me the best and be gentle with me. Give me the utmost of what I can handle and make me the fruit bearing tree, not the barren tree. As you give me, make me more humble. Let humility come with greatness, with having, not in renunciation. Many eons of time, Mother I have renounced on your behalf. Many eons of time I have let go of this world. I like the life of a hermit because I know it so well, but this lifetime Mother, let me have and let me become humble because I have. Let me become gentle and compassionate towards those who do not have, because I have so much. As you give me, help me share. Help me know what it is like not to be afraid of giving. Let me know what it is like not to want what someone else has, because what I have is greater and better and more and, in fact I can share it with everyone, with those that do not have as much as I have, without any fear that it will ever run out. Mother, I know you can give me and give me and give me and your resources are never ending. Your treasure house is always filled. You are the source of all Creation."

While you are in the Pool of Creation, take a deep breath and ask for what you want for your loved ones. On behalf of Earth and all humankind, ask for peace and harmony and love in all families. Ask for every human being to have enough food to eat, to have good shelter to sleep in, to have clothes that suit them. Ask for every human being to open themselves to the Divine Spark within their heart. Ask for those who have spiritually awakened to join you so you do not have to carry the burden alone. Ask for those who are newly awakened to reach a greater level of wakefulness and take on their responsibilities as your younger brothers and sisters in Light; to lighten your load, for you have carried this load for eons of time. Ask for those who are like you to join you so you do not feel lonely anymore. Ask for those who are a step ahead of you to also join you, to take you by the hand and walk ahead of you to make this path easier for you. Ask for the Masters to have greater health, greater stamina, greater strength, living and Ascended, most importantly the living Masters, the Avatars. Those who have made a sacrifice of their lives, those who travel across the world, sit for eighteen and twenty hours, to see, hug, hold and touch and awaken the multitudes and masses. Ask to earn the merit to see as many of them in this lifetime as possible. Say,

"Give me the merit, Mother, to be touched by the living Masters. Give me the merit to be touched by as many as my body and my being can handle. If I cannot be individually touched by each one, give me the merit to be energetically touched by them. Open me up to receive from all of them. Open me up to be in service to all of them and receive my prayers on behalf of all of them. Give them health, Mother. Give them greater power to serve the Light. Give them joy in their hearts. Let them feel rewarded for being here on Earth. Let their Light become stronger and more powerful so they can raise the Light on Earth, so they can awaken more souls, so they can guide the awakened souls, so they can accelerate all who are in their service and accept us as their disciples. Bring to us Mother, those who will teach us and guide us to the most accelerated and the most beneficial path of Light.

Remove from my path those who delay, distract, hurt, harm and abort me. My mission is a Divine Mission. Mother, I ask of you, give me the grace to serve my Divine Mission. I ask of you on behalf of all the members of my Soul Lineage of Light. I will perform ceremonies on any night or day and offer them in your honor Mother. Open up the doors of abundance and prosperity to me. Open up the doors of greater Light in my life, my hands, my body, and my being. Mother, show me your presence. Show me your grace. Show me your gifts. Let me know you have fully embraced me. From this moment on, walk ahead of me, and pave the path.

Walk by my side and hold my hand so that I know I am not alone. Walk behind me and push me forth, Mother. Carry me in your own heart. Carry me in your bosom, Mother. When I am tired and weary, when there are blisters on my feet, when I am afraid, when I think I have done something wrong, come to me and remind me to be gentle with myself. Remind me that I can do no wrong, that it is all an experience. Remind me that there are no mistakes, there are no failures, only experiences."

Pray for the Divine Mother. I teach you how to pray for her for she too needs prayers. The prayer that she needs is for her success in manifesting those designs and ideas which will anchor the energies of the Seed of the Pure and Innocent Feminine Child on Earth. As we move into the Seventh Golden Age, we are paving the path for a new Seed Race to be planted.

This new Seed Race will have a 3,000 year gestation period at the end of which, we will be half way through the Seventh Golden Age. Then we will begin a 12,000 year cycle of life for this new seed race, bringing back the purity and innocence of the Feminine Child Aspect to Earth. The Male Child Aspect came to Earth through the last Seed Race and its energies were corrupted. As that male child grew up to become an adult, corruption took full force and darkness took over the race.

Now we are coming to the end of that Seed Race and the Masculine Energies must hand over the power to the Feminine. To apply the Energies of the Feminine, we must start planting the Seed of the Pure and Innocent Feminine Child back on Earth. This is the Divine Mother's project. Do you want to be a good child? Do you want to serve her? Then pray to her and pray for her. Light a candle and say,

"I light this candle for the Divine Mother and her project of seeding the Earth with the Seed of the Pure and Innocent Feminine Child. I ask for the grace to be instrumental in the anchoring of the Pure and Innocent Feminine Child."

Keep a white candle lit whenever you can with the above intention, from now until you leave this body. She needs you just as you need her. We all need her.

Through this, you do yourself and the generations after you, generations for at least another fifteen thousand years to come, a favor. Even that will become a platform for the following twelve thousand year cycle and the new Seed Race. If this Seed is not corrupted in fifteen thousand years then there is no need to fold that project. That project can simply give way to the next one; one that can take us further into the Light. Presently we are in the process of folding the previous project because it has not served us. We have to release the darkness and dross from Earth before we can anchor the Pure and Innocent Feminine Child. Say to her,

"Mother, let me help you. Show me how I can be of service to you." Visualize yourself in the Pool of Creation, facing Goddess Lakshmi. Say, *"Goddess Lakshmi, you are the Goddess of Abundance for both spiritual evolution and material possessions. I ask you to give me what serves me the best. Accelerate me on my path."* Now, with clear intent, tell her what you want for yourself. Then say, *"Give me this or better so I can serve the Light."* Take a deep breath and sit in the Pool of Creation with Goddess Lakshmi.

Blueprint for the Higher Alternate Reality

I call forth the Blueprint for the Highest Alternate Reality and the greatest Act of Service to be placed inside a seed by the Divine Mother. I ask for the Blueprint for the creation of all things, all places, all people, and all events that best serve you from this point on for the rest of your life and for the benefit of multitudes and masses, and everyone you touch. I ask the Divine Mother to call forth that Blueprint from the Pool of Creation.

Visualize yourself standing on a circular platform stretching over the Pool of Creation. She is standing there with you. Experience this unique and individual experience, receiving the Seed that carries a Blueprint and a Template. The Template becomes all the actions which will manifest in your life from this day on; all the events which will unfold like a red carpet before you; the circumstances, the synchronistic events, people, places, and things that are most effective and beneficial to be brought to you. On your behalf, I ask for the release of karma and karmic entanglements; the release of all energies that no longer serve you; the release of all people, places and things that are standing in your way of serving the Light.

Visualize that the Divine Mother is placing a Seed in your Cosmic Heart Chakra. The Seed can be as small as a mustard seed or as large as your fist or even larger. It is a Golden Seed with some etchings on it. The seed will form in the palm of her right hand. She places it on top of the Flame of God-Unity in the center of your Cosmic Heart. The Seed sits on top of the Flame and begins to be illuminated by the love emanating from the Eternal Flame of God-Unity. She places both palms of her hands directly over your Heart Chakra. Her left hand is over her right hand. Her right hand is touching your Heart and she blows the breath of life into her hands and into your Heart. Feel the warmth, love and joy begin to bubble inside you and you feel lightness in your body. The Seed is now planted and the Blueprint is lodged inside of you.

From this moment on, the DNA structure of your cells will be receptive to the information that is in this Seed. The Seed begins to download the information from the Blueprint and the Template into your body and being. You will absorb and bring that wisdom to the consciousness of your body, mind, emotions, soul and spirit. The memory of all which you need to do and the willpower with which to do it is restored to you. From this moment on you will begin to walk this path fully empowered. You will have power to control the Five Elements. The Alchemy of turning Base Metal into Gold is achieved by controlling and exerting power over the Five Elements. Then you can create anything. Then you can truly and fully serve the Light. Then you can share the riches of this world with the multitudes and masses. Then you can take the power from the hands of those who are serving themselves and put it in the hands of those who deserve to be served. Then you will truly walk the path of Light. Every moment of your life will be to empower the Light. You will be the Emissaries of the Lords of Light.

As one last intention, I will now ask on your behalf and on my own behalf for the return of the Seven Lords of Light and the Guardianship of Light to take the reign of Earth. From this moment on, we demand and command that all positions of leadership are to be held by the Lords of Light. All disciples of the Lords of Light will take their positions serving the multitudes and masses. If you choose to be among those disciples, say it now. Say it in your own words and pause for a moment.

It is time to return. We ask permission to leave the Pool of Creation. In the company of the Divine Mother, we return to the Throne of Absolute. We bow down before her Throne as she takes her seat upon her throne. Together we stand before her and pour our love upon her for a moment. We send her love and pray that the Seed of the Pure and Innocent Feminine Child is fully planted and anchored on Earth. If you wish to, you may say,

"Mother, give me the Seed of the Pure and Innocent Child. Place it over the Seed you have already placed in my Cosmic Heart. From this day on I carry

the Seed of the Pure and Innocent Feminine Child with me." Say it in your own words. Do it with your own will. Say it as you wish to say it.

Bowing down to the Divine Mother, we begin our descent. Spiraling down from the Throne of Absolute to the Throne of the Seven Lords of Light and the Maha Lord of Light, we bow before all Seven Lords of Light and the Maha Lord of Light and move down to the Throne of Paramatman. Merging into the Throne of Paramatman, we carry the Light of Paramatman down with us. We move to the Throne of the Undifferentiated Source, to merge into the Pure Light of that throne.

The energy of God, non-manifest, is carried in our Heart as we move down to the Throne of Ellah where Pure White Light begins to take form. We bless that throne as we spiral down to the Throne of God-Source; the Cobalt-Blue is emanating everywhere. We spiral further down to the Throne of YHWH and carry the Golden Light with us further down. This throne is important as it has opened itself up to Earth and all humankind. We are now connected directly to the I Am That I Am as our own Force, and are also connected to the Throne of YHWH. When you call upon the I Am That I Am, call upon YHWH as well.

The Throne of YHWH is carrying an enormous Light and responsibility at this present juncture of Earth's evolution. The responsibility of holding your own individualized God-Force is now with this throne. The presence of the I Am has moved down from the Throne of the I Am That I Am to be closer to those of you who are receptive. The I Am Presence has taken leave of the throne to lower its essence to sit at your Crown Chakra. Connecting to this individualized aspect of the I Am Presence is therefore easier for you now. You can now hear its voice as the voice of your own Higher Self more clearly. If you hear a voice in your head, ask, *"Who are you?"* and if that answer is, *"I am your Higher Self."* Then know this to be the presence of I Am speaking to you. Similarly, if you hear the voice and you say, *"Who are you."* and hear, *"I Am."* Then know that this is your Higher Self. Your Higher Self has now merged into the I Am.

Therefore YHWH has opened its seat of Light to encompass the Throne of the I Am That I Am. This is a great and amazing feat which has happened recently. It benefits those of you with higher Light as you are now fully merged into the Presence of the I Am That I Am. However, it will be a long while for the un-awakened souls to know, understand or reach a point to benefit from the energies of the Throne of YHWH. Even though the gateways to the throne are open, everyone has to reach a specific Quotient of Light before they can benefit from it.

YHWH is close to you right now. Energies of YHWH are showered upon you. Your Pillar of Light extends beyond the I Am That I Am to the Throne of YHWH, as a matter of course now. The Cord of Light which extends from the top of your head is naturally illuminated up to the Throne of YHWH. The higher thrones are available to you upon your request. You have to knock on those doors and ask to enter. The Throne of YHWH is wide open to you. The individualized aspect of your God-Self extends to YHWH. You are allowed to experience God in Form at the Throne of YHWH. The power for manifestation is more than doubled, in fact it is multiplied!

The full power of that throne is now behind you, imagine that! Not only the Throne of the I Am That I Am, but the Throne of YHWH is behind you now.

We bless the Throne of YHWH and ask for greater intercession of the Throne, for the Presence of YHWH, Yahoweh-EL, EL-Shaddai, and Metatron and all aspects of the energies of YHWH. Spiral down to the Presence of the I Am That I Am and visualize that the presence of I Am is spiraling down with you and seating itself inside of the Lotus of your Crown Chakra. Visualize a beautiful, Thousand Petaled Lotus wide open above your Crown Chakra. Brilliant White Light is emanating from this lotus and the presence of the I Am is seated inside. This is your Higher Self now. Bring your consciousness to your body. Allow your body and being to bathe in the Light that you have become.

I thank you for taking the time and making the effort. If you do nothing but sit for five minutes to meditate and take yourself to the Pool of Creation, you have blessed me. If you do nothing but remember what I have taught you, everyday, you have blessed me, the Divine Mother and all the Masters and you would have served the Light. Do what you can when you can and know that we all hold you in our hearts. In the presence of all the Thrones, in the presence of Christ Maitreya, Sanat Kumara, St. Germain, Master Jesus, Melchizedek, Ancient of Days, Thoth and Elyon, the Cosmic and Great Beings of Light, the Brotherhoods and the Sisterhoods of the White Lodge, the Divine Mother and all of her aspects, Quan Yin, Hecate, Isis, Pele, Athena, Mother Mary, Lady Nada, Goddess of Victory, Goddess of Liberty, Lakshmi, Saraswati, Durga, Kali and many, many more. In the presence of the Seven Mighty Elohim and the Seven Chohans, the

Seven Lords of Light and the Maha Lord of Light, I bid you good night and I hold you in my own heart.

I bid you love. I hold you in my own heart. I will stand by your side. Call me whenever you need me. Call me even when you do not need me. I will be there. Remember Metatron. Remember YHWH. Remember Yahoweh-EL, the Feminine Aspect of the Throne of YHWH. Remember EL-Shaddai, the Feminine Aspect of Metatron.

I am your very own Metatron. So it is.

"I call forth the Red Life Force Energy of Earth to return to the Purity and Innocence originally intended in the Divine Plan. I pray for Earth to be free from dross. I pray for the collective consciousness of all humankind to be free from dross."

Metatron

CHAPTER XII

Lakshmi – Metatron Abundance Grid

In this chapter we are offered an Abundance Ceremony to combine energies of the Divine Mother with the Golden Throne together with two candle grids. One is the Grid of Abundance which is given by Metatron on the occasion of the gateway portal day of 8/8/08. Here Metatron brought us before Lakshmi, the Goddess of Abundance and asked her to bestow abundance and prosperity to all recipients.

In the second grid I have combined the Abundance Magnification Grids of Metatron and Goddess Lakshmi with the grid of Goddess Hecate and 13 aspects of Divine Mother. Magnification Grids are extremely powerful. There are three components to a Magnification Grid. The first is the candles. When charged, candles can carry the energy of a specific thing or a certain quality. The second is the crystals which magnify the intentions for the Grid and add acceleration. The third is the intercession of the Great Beings invoked to add their powerful energies to the Grid. In this Grid, we call upon thirteen mighty aspects of the Divine Mother. The sequence in this Candle Grid of Light is that the candles empower the crystals. The crystals magnify the intention for the grid and the power and might of the thirteen Goddesses further accelerate our intentions. The Divine Mother has decreed to provide for all our mundane needs, especially to bring financial prosperity and abundance through this grid.

If you are unable to physically make any one of these candle grids, please do not be discouraged. Metatron has taught us that it is equally as potent, perhaps even more effective, to visualize any one of these candle grids and offer it to the Masters in the Altar of our hearts.

Simply visualize the entire process, step by step, by imagining that the candle grid is set up in the Palace of your Heart. Each day focus on the grid in your heart and meditate for a few minutes to keep the energy of the grid active.

We have all been called to become Beacons of Light, receiving and anchoring the energies of the Divine Mother and the abundance of the Universe. Through the Grace of all the Thrones and with the blessing of all the Masters we will succeed in this endeavor, together in Oneness.

I wish you a wonderful, prosperous and abundant journey into the Realms of Light in the company of the Divine Mother and all the Masters.

Magnification Candle Grid of Abundance

Beloveds of my own heart, I am Metatron.

I bring you a very potent Candle Grid of Abundance with Goddess Lakshmi and the Throne of YHWH. Light this Grid for at least twenty-two days. It will bring you accelerated abundance.

Material Needed

- White Poster Board
- Gold Pen
- 4 White candles
- 1 Red candle
- 1 Gold candle (yellow may be used if gold is not available)
- One double terminated crystal or crystal cluster

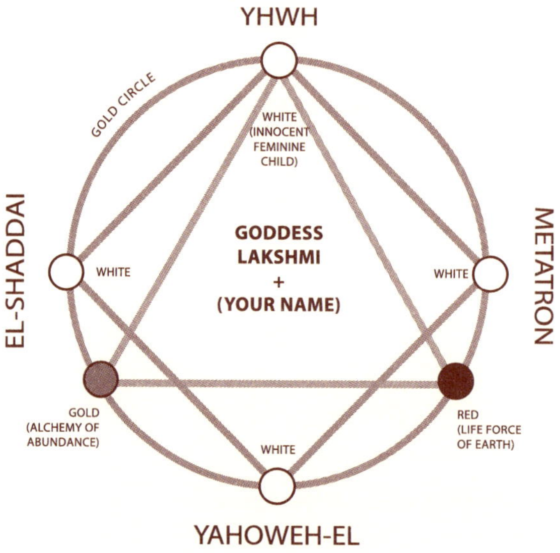

Setting Up the Candle Grid

- Draw the Grid as shown in the diagram, with the gold pen. The three points of the triangle will touch the gold circle. The gold circle is the epitome of the manifestation of all that serves you. This circle is a bubble which holds the Seed of the ultimate Creative Force that will serve you and will help you to serve.
- Write the name of Goddess Lakshmi along with your name in the center. Write the names of YHWH at North, EL-Shaddai at the position West, Yahoweh-EL at South and Metatron at East.
- Place the crystal in the center over your name and that of Goddess Lakshmi.
- Place the first white candle at the top of the triangle where the square and triangle share the same point. Place

the red and gold candles at the other two points of the triangle. Place the other three white candles at the remaining three points of the square.

Lighting and Charging the Candles

- To charge the white candle, pick it up; hold it in your raised hands and say,

  "I charge this white candle with the energy of purity and innocence from the Seed of the Pure and Innocent Female Child, from the Heart of the Divine Mother and I pray for that Purity and Innocence to return to Earth." Say this three times. Place the candle down.

- Lift up the red candle and say,

  "I call forth the Red Life Force Energy of Earth to return to the Purity and Innocence originally intended in the Divine Plan. I pray for Earth to be free from dross. I pray for the collective consciousness of all humankind to be free from dross." Say this three times. Place the candle down.

- Lift up the gold candle and say,

  "I call the alchemy of the Heavenly Realms, and the Creative Force of the Divine Mother to bring to me the ability to change base metal into gold and to have control over the Five Elements." Say this three times. Place the candle down.

- Moving clockwise, pick up the white candle shared by the Pure and Innocent Feminine Child and the Throne of YHWH and say,

  "I ask the Throne of YHWH to imbue, embody, protect and guide my body and being with the energies and the Light of YHWH."

- Pick up the white candle of Metatron and say,
  "I ask Metatron to imbue, embody, protect and guide my body and my being with the energies and the Light of Metatron."
- Pick up the white candle for Yahoweh-EL and say,
  "I ask Yahoweh-EL to imbue, embody, protect and guide my body and my being with the energies and the Light of Yahoweh-EL."
- Pick up the white candle for EL-Shaddai and say,
  "I ask EL-Shaddai to imbue, embody, protect and guide my body and being with the energies and the Light of EL-Shaddai."

Every time you light your candle grid, visualize yourself and Goddess Lakshmi at the center of that grid. Lighting the candles will magnify your intentions. The crystals will add to the magnification. What matters is your intention. Intend it and hold the intention in your heart and it will be just as good.

Any crystal will work. I ask you to carry around double terminated, clear quartz crystals. These will hold the energy of the Seed, the Seed of the manifestation of the reality which is most beneficially ordained by the Divine Mother for you. When you hold your double terminated crystal, visualize that the Seed is activating it. Holding it in your hand while you meditate will continue to magnify the impact of the Seed that is in your Heart. If you do not have a double terminated crystal, take any crystal and ask the Divine Mother to charge it. She specifically asks you to work with clear quartz clusters to represent the many aspects of the Divine Mother.

Call upon the Divine Mother and ask her to charge your clusters and to imbue your clusters with the Seed. Make your abundance candle grids using these crystals. When you are meditating, you can take your crystal out of the Abundance Candle Grid, hold it in your hand and sit with it. When you are not meditating, put it in your candle grid. Light the candle grid and let the crystal magnify the impact of the candles and the candles magnify the impact of your intentions.

Remember Metatron. Remember YHWH. Remember Yahoweh-EL, the Feminine Aspect of the Throne of YHWH. Remember EL-Shaddai, the Feminine Aspect of Metatron. I bid you love. I hold you in my own heart. I will stand by your side. Call me whenever you need me. Call me even when you do not need me. I will be there.

I hold you in my own heart. I am your very own Metatron. So it is.

Hecate - Divine Mother Grid Combined With Lakshmi - Metatron Magnification Grid of Abundance

This is a grid which combines the Abundance Magnification Grids of Metatron and Goddess Lakshmi with the Grid of Goddess Hecate and thirteen Aspects of Divine Mother, previously given in Chapter XII of *Path to Enlightenment, Book II.* The energies of both of these Grids are important. The combined forces of the two grids will increase the potency of both and accelerate the outcome. The twenty-two or thirty day period for full anchoring for greater acceleration, is therefore, of utmost importance. I recommend a longer term exercise of this grid; to over a three to six month period of time. Simply having the presence of all the feminine Deities through the activation of this candle grid is an enormous blessing.

As both Metatron and Divine Mother reiterate, manifesting abundance and prosperity is an important pillar for our spiritual evolution and for acceleration of our Divine Mission. During the time of Solstice and Equinox, the energies are intensified and portals of energetic exchange with the Higher Realms are wide open. Performing this Magnification Candle Grid for the twenty-two days can be powerful. Repeating the Grid of Light exercise ceremony for the entire month can add momentum and acceleration to all your endeavors.

Hecate – Divine Mother Grid Combined with Lakshmi – Metatron Grid

Materials Needed

- Choose one of the following colors for your poster board: White, red, black or yellow.
- Gold or Blue Pen
- 17 White votives or tea lights
- 1 large pillar White candle
- 1 large pillar Red candle
- 1 large pillar Gold candle (yellow may be used if gold is not available)
- 1 large pillar Black candle
- One double terminated crystal or crystal cluster
- One piece of gold, gold jewelry or gold colored coin
- Cinnamon

Setting up the Candle Grid

- Draw the Grid as shown in the diagram, with the gold or blue pen.
- Write the name of Goddess Lakshmi along with your name in the center.
- At the four corners of one square, write the name of YHWH at twelve o'clock, Metatron at the position of three o'clock, Yahoweh-EL at six o'clock and EL-Shaddai at nine o'clock, as shown in the diagram.
- At the four corners of the other square, write the names of Lakshmi, Saraswati, Durga and Kali as shown on the diagram.

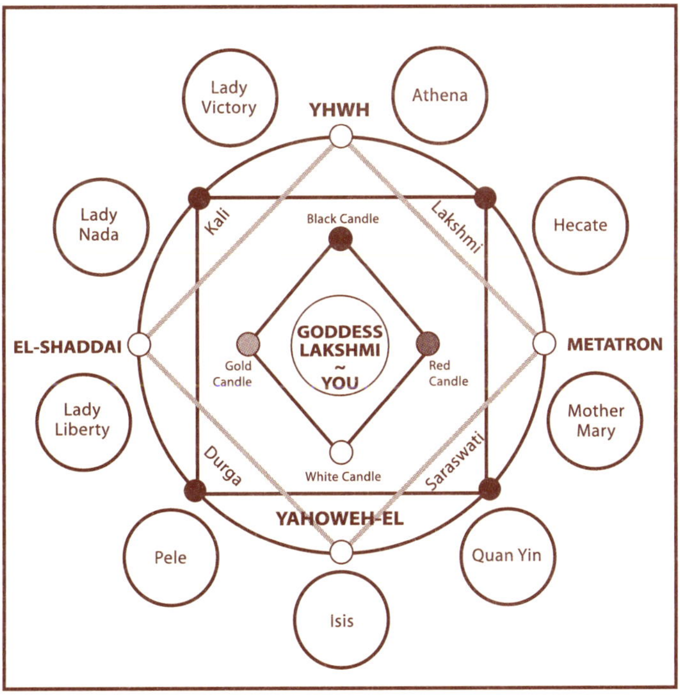

- Around the circle write the names of Lady Victory, Athena, Hecate, Mother Mary, Quan Yin, Isis, Pele, Lady Liberty and Lady Nada.
- Place a mound of cinnamon in the center of the yin yang symbol over the names of you and Goddess Lakshmi. Place a piece of gold over the mound and place the crystal over that.
- Place your four pillar candles at the four points of the diamond shape. Refer to the diagram for color placement.
- Place a votive or tea candle at the four points of the square with the four aspects of the Throne of YHWH.
- Place a votive or tea candle over all the names of Divine Mother (you should have 13 tea candle placements all together).
- Sprinkle cinnamon around the entire large circle covering the line that you drew.

Lighting and Charging the Candles

- Pick up the black candle, hold it up and say,

  "I call forth the transmutation forces of Heaven and Earth to remove all darkness from my life and my being. Release and remove all obstacles from my path of abundance and prosperity and accelerate the manifestation of all beneficial resources into my life and my hands. I ask the Divine Mother to transmute all negativity and all obstacles from my path of abundance and prosperity." Place the candle back on the grid.
- Pick up the Red candle, hold it up and say,

"I call forth the Red Life Force from the Earthly Realms to fill my life and my hands with the abundance and prosperity, passion and strength, wealth, health and comfort. I ask Goddess Gaia to imbue this candle grid with the Life Force and treasures of Earth." Place the candle back on the grid.

- Pick up the White candle; hold it up and say,

  "I call forth the Pure and Innocent Feminine Child aspect. I ask the Divine Mother to imbue this candle with the Seed of the Pure and Innocent Feminine Child. I ask the Divine Mother to fill this Candle Grid with the abundance and prosperity of the Creative Force." Place the white candle back on the grid.

- Pick up the Gold candle, hold it up and say,

  "I call forth the Alchemy of the Heavenly Realms, to bring abundance and prosperity from higher dimensions to fill my life and my hands. I ask Divine Mother to fill this candle grid with the limitless abundance of the Heavenly Realms." Place the gold candle back on the Grid.

- Now go to the four aspects of the YHWH Throne; YHWH, Metatron, Yahoweh-EL and EL-Shaddai. Going clockwise, pick up each votive or tea candle and do the following:

- Pick up the first candle and say,

  "I ask the Throne of YHWH to imbue, embody, protect and guide my body and being with the energies and the Light of YHWH." Place the candle back on the grid.

- Pick up the second candle and say,

  "I ask Metatron to imbue, embody, protect and guide my body and my being with the energies and the Light of Metatron."

Place the candle back on the grid.

- Pick up the third candle and say,

  "I ask Yahoweh-EL to imbue, embody, protect and guide my body and my being with the energies and the Light of Yahoweh-EL." Place the candle back on the grid.

- Pick up the fourth candle and say,

  "I ask EL-Shaddai to imbue, embody, protect and guide my body and being with the energies and the Light of EL-Shaddai." Place the candle back on the grid.

- Now go to the four Goddesses; Lakshmi, Saraswati, Durga and Kali, around the square. One by one, pick up the votive or tea candle and say,

  "I call forth Goddess (name of Goddess) to bring forth (state your intention)." Place each candle back in its position.

- Now go to each of the 9 Goddesses around the circle and pick up each candle in turn and say, *"I call forth Goddess (name of Goddess) to bring forth (state intention)."* Place each candle back in its position.

- Once all candles are imbued and placed back in their positions, you may begin to light them. Start by lighting from inside out. First light the four pillars, then the Throne of YHWH, then the four Goddesses around the square, then the Nine Goddesses around the circle. Sit and meditate for a few minutes to anchor the energies of your candle grid.

When the votives burn out, start new candles and make new intentions or gain momentum with the same intentions. Print all your intentions on a piece of paper and place them by the Candle Grid and say them each time you light the Grid.

Abundance Ceremony to Combine Energies of Divine Mother with the Golden Throne

My Children of Light, I am Hecate.

Envision yourself standing in the center of the grid facing Goddess Lakshmi. Visualize yourself beginning to spin around her. You spin faster and faster and implode, merging into the being of Goddess Lakshmi. The implosion becomes an explosion of Golden Light that forms a Golden Sphere around you and Goddess Lakshmi. While in the Golden Sphere, set out your personal and global intentions.

Visualize yourself standing at the Throne of YHWH, with the presence of YHWH at twelve o'clock, EL-Shaddai at three o'clock,

Yahoweh-EL at six o'clock and Metatron at nine o'clock. Visualize that the Golden Sphere with you and Lakshmi expands, imploding and merging into the four beings around the Throne. The implosion becomes an explosion of Golden Light which forms a larger Golden Sphere around you and Goddess Lakshmi. While in the Golden Sphere, once again, set out your personal and global intentions.

Visualize the circle expanding to encompass all aspects of the Divine Mother; you and Lakshmi with Saraswati, Durga, Kali, Athena, Hecate, Mother Mary, Quan Yin, Isis, Pele, Lady Liberty, Lady Nada and Lady Victory. Pause, bathe in the Golden Light, and state your intentions.

You may perform this meditation by drawing a circle physically outside in the sand, or inside in a room and stand inside the circle with Goddess Lakshmi.

Perform this candle grid ceremony every day and as many times as you can. You may look up the important portal and energy days, 9/9, 9/18, Fall Equinox, September 19-22, 9/24 and 9/27. For whatever point in the year you choose to perform these grids and ceremonies. You may visit www.wavesofbliss.com to find out important portal days and for current planetary events from the point of view of the Masters.

May your path be cleared of all your obstacles, your mind illuminated with Light and your heart blessed with the joy of serving the Light and being the Light of this world.

I am your mother Hecate. So it is. Blessed be.

Channeling Index

Chapter I: Protection Grid of Light
October 2008 Newsletter
Divine Mother, channeled September 21, 2008

Chapter II: Healing and Protection
February 2008 Newsletter
Metatron, channeled on January 11, 2008

Chapter III: Soul Lineage of Light
March 2008 Newsletter
Melchizedek, channeled January 14, 2008

Chapter IV: Sphere of Remembrance
April 2008 Newsletter
St. Germain, channeled January 29, 2008

Chapter V: Power, Purity, Love,
Protection and Healing
May 2008 Newsletter
Hecate, Quan Yin and Mother Mary, channeled January 16, 2008

Chapter VI: Hope, Creativity and Happiness
June Newsletter
Quan Yin and Archangel Ariel, channeled May 14, 2008

Chapter VII: Empowerment and Purity
July Newsletter
Sanat Kumara and Thoth, channeled May 12, 2008

Chapter VIII: Sphere of Illumination and Flame of God-Unity
St. Germain, channeled January 15, 2008

Chapter IX: Manifestation
May Newsletter
Hecate, channeled January 16, 2008

Chapter X: Life in Service to Christ Maitreya
November Newsletter
Sanat Kumara, Metatron and Hecate, channeled February 12, 2008

Chapter XI: Journey to the Thrones
Metatron, channeled August 8, 2008

Chapter XII: Lakshmi – Metatron Abundance Grid
Magnification Candle Grid
August (8/8/08) Special Edition Newsletter
Metatron, channeled August 8, 2008

Hecate – Divine Mother Grid
Combined with Lakshmi – Metatron Grid
September 2008 Newsletter (combined Hecate and Metatron grids)

Organization Websites for Related Information

www.nasrinsafai.com

www.wavesofbliss.com

www.share-international.org

www.waynepeterson.com

www.karunamayi.org

www.amma.org

www.mmdarshanamerica.com

www.yantradesigngroup.com

www.edgarcayce.org

www.PTEAcademy.org

Bibliography

Alper, Frank. *Exploring Atlantis, Vol I.* Adamis International, Inc., 1987.

Andrews, Shirley. *Lemuria and Atlantis: Studying the Past to Survive the Future.* Llewellyn Worldwide, LTD., 2004.

Bolton, Leslie. *The Everything Classic Mythology Book.* Avon, Massachusetts: Adams Media Corporation. 2002.

Charles, R.H., Translated. *Book of Enoch.* 1917.

Charlton, Hilda. *Hell Bent on Heaven.* Woodstock, New York: Golden Quest. 1990.

Charlton, Hilda. *Master Hilarion.* Woodstock, New York: Golden Quest. 1995.

Chodron, Pema. *When Things Fall Apart.* Boston, MA: Shamballa Publications, Inc., 1997.

Doreal. *The Emerald Tablets of Thoth the Atlantean.* Source Books, Inc., 2002.

Englebert, Omer. *The Lives of the Saints.* Translated by Christopher and Ann Fremantle. New York: Barnes and Noble Books. 1994.

Freke, Timothy and Gandy, Peter. *The Hermetica: The Lost Wisdom of the Pharaohs.* Jeremy P. Torcher/Penguin Putnam Inc., 1997.

Guiley, Rosemary. *Encyclopedia of the Strange, Mystical & Unexplained.* Random House Value Publishing, 2001.

Guiley, Rosemary Ellen. *Encyclopedia of Angels. 2nd Edition.* Checkmark Books, 2004.

Guiley, Rosemary and Kraig, Donald. *Encyclopedia of Magic & Alchemy.* Facts on File, Inc., 2006.

Guiley, Rosemary and Kraig, Donald. *Encyclopedia of Saints.*

Haich, Elisabeth. *Initiation.* Aurora Press, Incorporated, 2000.

Hendricks, Rhoda. *Classical Gods and Heroes, Myths as Told by Ancient Authors.* New York: Harper Collins Publishers, 2004.

Kaplan, Aryeh. *Sefer Yetzirah: The Book of Creation.* Rev. ed. Samuel Weiser, 1997.

Khan, M.Z. Translated. *Quran.* Interlink Publishing Group, Inc., 1997.

Lockman Foundation. *Amplified Bible.* Zondervan, 1987.

Luk, A.D.K. *Law of Life, Books I and II.* A.D.K. Publications, 1960.

McBrien, Richard P. *Lives of the Saints from Mary and St. Francis of Assisi to John XXIII and Mother Teresa.* New Yok: Harper Collins, 2001.

Millman, Dan. *The Life You Were Born To Live: A Guide to Finding Your Life Purpose.* California: New World Library, 1993.

Myss, Caroline. *Entering the Castle.* New York: Free Press, 2007.

Plato. *Timaeus and Critias.* New York: Oxford World's Classics, 2008.

Prophet, Mark and Elizabeth Clare. *Lords of the Seven Rays.* Corwin Springs Montana: Summit University Press, 1986.

Reid, Vera W. *Towards Aquarius.* London: Aquarian Press, 1969.

Safai, Nasrin. *Gifts from the Masters of Light: Journeys Into the Inner Realms of Consciousness – Gifts III.* Waves of Bliss Publishing, 2005.

SMVA Trust. *Sri. Karunamayi: A Biography.* SMVA Trust, Inc., 2005.

Springett, Bernard. *Zoroaster: The Great Teacher.* Rider, 1923.

Sri. Karunamayi, Amma. *Blessed Souls: The Teachings of Sri. Karunamayi, Vol. I.* SMVA Trust, Inc., 1999.

Sri. Karunamayi, Amma. *Blessed Souls: The Teachings of Sri. Karunamayi, Vol. II.* SMVA Trust, Inc., 2000.

Wilbur, Ken. *A Brief History of Everything.* Shambhala Publications, 1996.

Acknowledgements

I offer joy and deep gratitude to the Divine Mother for her presence in my life and in the lives of all her children who are affected by this book.

I thank the following contributors for allowing the Divine Mother to bring this book into life with their help:

To Patsy Balacchi of Yantra Design Group for her expertise in book design, cover art, typography and for her insistence to bring perfection, in honor and love of the Divine Mother,

To my friend and co-traveler on the Path of Light, Kathy Rowshan, for her diligent and disciplined work in compilation of the drafts, reviews, proofs and formatting as well as her contributions in compilation of electronic sound and text files and for many hours of selfless service for the Waves of Bliss website,

To Jane A. Matthews for her publishing and editing skills,

To James Foster and Tonia Pinheiro for transcriptions, diagram designs and reviews,

To Theresa Martin for diagram design,

To Sunny Alavi, Geert De Vuyst, Allen Blanchard, Myan Spear and Hara Weaver for reviews of the final drafts,

To Dr. John Alderson and Shabnam Sadr for their loving support,

To all those who participated in receiving and anchoring the channeled materials compiled in this book and all whose lives are affected by reading them.

About the Author

Nasrin Safai is an internationally known lecturer in the field of esoteric spirituality. Author of seven channeled books in the field of metaphysics, she brings messages from the realms of the Spiritual Masters, Guides and Angels. The Universal Laws, as explained by the Masters, bring a new perspective to the understanding of metaphysics as applied to our daily life. She offers life and soul bridge readings to aid those who are drawn to find their greater purpose in life and their life's mission. In addition to private sessions, Nasrin also conducts Public Group Channeling sessions where hundreds of people gather from around the world via conference call.

Part of Nasrin's life's mission is to travel the world anchoring Ascension Energies of Light at locations on all continents through ceremonies, sacred dances, mantras, prayers and invocations given by the Masters. Nasrin has been a channel for Divine Mother, Metatron, Melchizedek, Sanat Kumara, Archangel Michael, Uriel, Raphael, Jesus, Mother Mary, Buddha, St. Germain, Quan Yin, Hecate, Athena, Red Feather and other Ascended Beings of Light.

Nasrin attended Chelsea School of Art in London, received a Bachelors Degree from the University of Decorative Arts in Tehran, a Masters Degree in Environmental Planning from Nottingham University in England and did her Doctoral Studies in the role of women in the development of the third world. She has taught at Harvard University and universities and institutes of higher education around the world. Presently she holds the post of Professor of Esoteric Spirituality at Universal Seminary, where materials from her books are taught for college credit.

Nasrin is the founder of the Foundation for the Attainment of God-Unity (FAGU), an educational and holistic organization which provides classes, workshops, books and support materials for spiritual practice, open to all. All proceeds from the sale of this book support the work of the Masters through FAGU (www.godunity.org).

Other Books by Nasrin Safai

Path to Enlightenment: The Pillar of Light, Book I.
Waves of Bliss Publishing, 2008.

Path to Enlightenment: The Golden Throne, Book II.
Waves of Bliss Publishing, 2008.

Gifts from Ascended Beings of Light:
Prayers, Meditation, Mantra and Journeys for Soul Growth – Gifts I.
Agapi Publishing, 2003.

Gifts of Practical Guidance for Daily Living:
Healing, Protection, Manifestation, Enlightenment – Gifts II.
Waves of Bliss Publishing, 2005.

Gifts from the Masters of Light:
Journeys Into the Inner Realms of Consciousness – Gifts III.
Waves of Bliss Publishing, 2005.

Gifts of Wisdom and Truth from the Masters of Light:
Tools for Clearing, Release, Abundance and Empowerment – Gifts IV.
Waves of Bliss Publishing, 2005.

To purchase a book, visit www.wavesofbliss.com/shop/categories/Books or email Nasrin@wavesofbliss.com.

To subscribe to our free newsletter, go to www.wavesofbliss.com.